Culinary Arts Institute

ITALIAN COOKBOOK

Featured in cover photo:
a. **Baked Shrimp,** 16
b. **Cream Rolls,** 49
c. **Meat-Stuffed Manicotti,** 38

ITALIAN

ITALIAN COOKBOOK

The Culinary Arts Institute Staff:

Helen Geist: Director
Sherrill Corley: Editor
Barbara MacDonald: Contributing Editor • Helen Lehman: Assistant Editor
Charlotte Costantini, Mary Ann Michels: Consultants
Edward Finnegan: Executive Editor • Charles Bozett: Art Director
Ethel La Roche: Editorial Assistant • Ivanka Simatic: Recipe Tester
Malinda Miller: Copy Editor • John Mahalek: Art Assembly

Book designed and coordinated by Charles Bozett and Laurel DiGangi

Illustrations by Ralph Creasman

Cover photo: Bob Scott Studios   Inside photos: Zdenek Pivecka

Adventures in Cooking SERIES

COOKBOOK

Culinary Arts Institute

1727 South Indiana, Chicago, Illinois 60616

Contents

The History of Italian Cuisine

A coin tossed into the Fountain of Trevi promises the visitor a return visit to Rome. This fountain is widely used on travel posters, and it is a fitting symbol for Italy, fountainhead for so much of the world's culture. Religion, painting, sculpture, and opera have all reached their zenith here, and left monuments that draw students the world over.

Food ranks high among Italy's contributions. Even the vocabulary we use to discuss cooking has Roman origins. The word for "recipe" and many other cooking terms have Latin roots.

Italian cooking has been centuries in the making and is distinctively different from other European cuisines. It reflects the personality of the Italian people, and the historic events that have shaped their lives.

Modern Italy traces its ancestry to the Roman Empire, and to the tribes of Latins, Romans, Greeks, and Etruscans who populated the land before the Empire. These people scraped together a livelihood from farming and sheepherding, for the most part.

Getting enough food to sustain life was more difficult than we can imagine from the vantage point of our Supermarket Age. Finding a staple such as salt, for example, was a real challenge for the early Romans. They met it by devising a way to dehydrate sea water. Their inventiveness not only met their need for salt, but started them on a lucrative salt trade with their neighbors. To say a man was "worth his salt" in those days was no small compliment.

Man needed his daily bread then as now, too, but the form in which he made it would be unrecognizable by today's standards. It was called "puls," and it was made from whatever grain was available. For the early Romans, this was often millet. The grain was ground and mixed with liquid to make a mush. This could be eaten warm as a sort of cooked cereal, or allowed to harden into a cake. Puls is said to have been the ration of the Roman soldier, and whatever it lacked in esthetics was compensated for by its nourishing qualities.

Up until about two hundred years before Christ, breadmaking was done at home. At that time, bakeries began to appear in the marketplace. A few can be found among the ruins at Pompeii.

Cheese has always played a major role in Italian cooking. The ancients made theirs in a form similar to cottage cheese. Since sheep were readily available, the cheese was made from ewes' milk.

The hardships of life in early Rome were softened by the presence of wine, as wine making dates back to as early as 2400 B.C. in Egypt. The Etruscans introduced the art to Rome. Wine making is still important in the life and economy of Italy.

The curtain went up on the Roman Empire in 27 B.C., when Augustus became the first emperor. The Empire at its greatest extent stretched from Spain and the British Isles on the west to Asia Minor in the east, and included northern Africa. Cooking, like all aspects of culture, was both carried to the conquered lands and brought back from them.

The subject of food during the Roman Empire evokes scenes of lavish feasting with platters heaped high with culinary creations. Such affairs took place, we learn from poets and historians, but were far from commonplace. The average Roman had to settle for life's essentials.

The literature of the early Roman Empire also tells us that the modern Italian appreciation for vegetables, and perhaps some understanding of nutrition, has early roots. In the first century B.C., Cato the Censor became one of the earliest exponents of good nutrition on record when he preached the merits of cabbage. Despite his lack of scientific data, he was close to the mark. Cabbage is a relatively good source of vitamin C. Providing a daily source of this vitamin was essential at a time when dried and cooked cereals, notably lacking in vitamin C, were the mainstay of the diet.

Those who couldn't afford cabbage often made do with boiled greens, also known now to be rich in nutritional value. A variety of chard and a plant called mallow were prepared much as spinach is prepared today. The fava bean was widely used, too.

As trade with distant countries developed during the time of the Empire, a taste for fruit was cultivated. Peaches and melons were introduced from Persia and apricots from Armenia. Apples ceased to be a rarity, and Lucullus, who gave his name to "Lucullan feasts," introduced the cherry. Dates were brought in from Africa. Together, these fruits provided a panorama of flavor and color that still beautifies the Roman table.

Early Rome did have a supermarket of sorts. It was named for the emperor Trajan, who ruled from A.D. 98 to 117. It was a multilevel market, set up on the slope of the Quirinal, one of Rome's famous seven hills. At the hub of the market was a semicircle of arched doorways that led into some of the shops; others set up booths in the open air. The wine merchant, butcher, baker, and fishmonger all hawked their wares. Shoppers pushed their way through the crowd, carrying the baskets and jugs that held their purchases.

The glory that once was Rome—and all of Italy—can add luster to your table. This *Italian Cookbook* is in part arranged by region, with recipes grouped according to their place of origin. Naturally, they overlap somewhat, but they are placed where one is most apt to find them served in Italy. This collection will help you design a meal that is true to the original, and that will give a new dimension to both family and company meals. *Buon appetito!*

Glossary

acciughe (ah-CHEW-gay)—anchovies

aceto (ah-CHAY-toe)—vinegar

aglio (AHL-yo)—garlic

agnello (ahn-YEYL-lo)—lamb

al dente (ahl DEN-tay)—term for not quite tender pasta; literally "to the tooth"

al forno (ahl FORR-no)—baked

amaretti (ah-mah-RRAY-tee)—macaroons

ananasso (ah-nah-NAHS-so)—pineapple

antipasto (ahn-tee-PAH-stoe)—first course, usually served cold

aragosta (ah-rrah-GAW-stah)—lobster

arancine (ah-rrahn-CHEE-nay)—fried rice balls; literally "little oranges"

asparagi (ah-SPARR-ah-jee)—asparagus

Asti Spumante (AH-stee spoo-MAHN-tay)—sparkling white wine from the Piedmont

baccalà (bah-kah-LAH)—cod

Bel Paese (bel pah-EY-zay)—soft ripened, mild cheese with creamy texture; originated in Lombardy

biscotti (bee-SKAW-tee)—biscuits or cookies

bistecca (bee-STAY-kah)—beefsteak

brodetto (brraw-DEY-toe)—fish soup

brodo (BRRAW-doe)—broth

burro (BOO-rroe)—butter

cacciatore (kah-chah-TOE-rray)—food, usually chicken, prepared in a spicy tomato sauce; literally "hunter"

caciocavallo (kah-choe-kah-VAHL-loe)—a hard ripened, firm cheese with piquant flavor

caffè (kah-FEH)—coffee

calamari (kah-lah-MAH-rree)—baby squid

canederli (kah-nay-DEYRR-lee)—soup dumplings

cannelloni (kah-nay-LOE-nee)—usually flat squares of pasta rolled around a stuffing to form tubular pasta; literally "large reeds"

cannoli (kah-NO-lee)—deep-fried pastry tubes filled with sweet ricotta mixture

caponata (kah-poe-NAH-tah)—relish made of eggplant and other vegetables

cappelletti (kah-pay-LAY-tee)—moist, stuffed pasta usually served in soup; literally "little hats"

capperi (KAH-pay-rree)—capers

carciofi (kahrr-CHAW-fee)—artichokes

carote (kah-RRAW-tay)—carrots

cavolfiore (kah-voel-FYOE-rray)—cauliflower

Chianti (kee-YAHN-tee)—a dry, red wine

cipolle (chee-POEL-lay)—onions

conchigliette (cone-keel-YAY-tay)—tiny shells of pasta

costolette (coe-stoe-LAY-tay)—cutlets or chops

crostini (crroe-STEE-nee)—toasted bread

ditalini (dee-tah-LEE-nee)—tubular-shaped pasta about ¼ inch in both diameter and length; usually served in soup

fagioli (fah-JOE-lee)—beans

fagiolini (fah-joe-LEE-nee)—green beans

fegato (FAY-gah-toe)—liver

fettuccine (fay-too-CHEE-nay)—noodles about ¼ inch wide

finocchio (fee-NAWK-yo)—anise-flavored celerylike vegetable; also known as fennel

fonduta (foen-DOO-tah)—cheese fondue

fontina (foen-TEE-nah)—creamy, soft cheese with slight nutlike flavor

formaggio (forr-MAH-joe)—cheese

fragole (FRRAH-go-lay)—strawberries

frittata (frree-TAH-tah)—omelet

fritto (FRREE-toe)—fried

frutta (FRROO-tah)—fruit

funghi (FOON-ghee)—mushrooms

gamberetti (gahm-bay-RRAY-tee)—shrimp

gelato (jay-LAH-toe)—frozen; refers to ice cream or sherbet

gnocchi (n-YAW-kee)—dumplings made of semolina or potato flour dough, shaped, and either poached or baked

Gorgonzola (gorr-goen-ZOE-lah)—semisoft, blue-veined cheese with tangy flavor; from Lombardy

granita (grrah-NEE-tah)—sherbet

grissini (grree-SEE-nee)—breadsticks

imbottitura (eem-boe-tee-TOO-rrah)—stuffing

insalata (een-sah-LAH-tah)—salad

lasagne (lah-ZAHN-yay)—broad, flat noodle about 1½ inches wide

lasagnette (lah-zahn-YAY-tay)—flat noodle about ½ to ¾ inch wide

latte (LAH-tay)—milk

legumi (lay-GOO-mee)—vegetables

lenticchie (len-TEEK-yay)—lentils

limone (lee-MOE-nay)—lemon

linguine (leen-GWEE-nay)—a narrow, flat noodle about ⅛ inch thick; literally "little tongues"

lumachine (loo-mah-KEE-nay)—small snail-shaped pasta

maccheroni (mah-kay-RROE-nee)—macaroni

maiale (mah-YAH-lay)—pork

manicotti (mah-nee-KAW-tee)—large rectangles of pasta dough rolled around a stuffing; also, large pasta tubes, about 4 inches long and 1 inch in diameter

marinara (mah-rree-NAH-rrah)—quick, spicy tomato sauce prepared with a few ingredients such as a sailor would have at his disposal

Marsala (mahrr-SAHL-ah)—fortified, amber-colored wine; either dry or sweet

melanzana (may-lahn-ZAH-nah)—eggplant

mele (MAY-lay)—apples

melone (may-LOE-nay)—melon

minestrone (mee-nes-TRROE-nay)—thick vegetable soup; sometimes contains meat

mostaccioli (moe-stah-CHAW-lee)—a hollow, tubular pasta cut obliquely, about 2½ inches long

mozzarella (moet-sah-RREL-lah)—a fresh, unsalted, moist white cheese with a delicate flavor

olio (AWL-yo)—oil

oregano (oh-RRAY-gah-no)—herb of mint family; widely used in Italian cookery

palombacci (pah-loem-BAH-chee)—wild pigeons

pane (PAH-nay)—bread

panettone (pah-nay-TOE-nay)—Christmas fruit bread

parmigiáno (pahrr-mee-JOHN-oh)—Parmesan cheese

pasta (PAH-stah)—dough composed chiefly of flour, water, and sometimes eggs, and made into a wide variety of shapes and sizes of spaghetti, macaroni, and noodles

patate (pah-TAH-tay)—potatoes

peperoni (pay-pay-RROE-nee)—sweet red or green peppers

pesce (PAY-shay)—fish

piccante (pee-KAHN-tay)—piquant

pignoli (peen-YAW-lee)—pine nuts

piselli (pee-ZEL-lee)—peas

pizza (PEET-sah)—open-face tomato-cheese pie

pizzaiola (peet-sah-YAW-lah)—"pizza style"; with piquancy and sharpness

polenta (poe-LEN-tah)—cornmeal mush

pollo (PAWL-lo)—chicken

polpette (poel-PAY-tay)—meatballs

pomodoro (poe-moe-DAW-rroe)—tomatoes

porco (PAWRR-ko)—pork

prosciutto (prroe-SHOO-toe)—Italian-style ham pressed and aged in spices

provolone (prroe-voe-LOE-nay)—hard ripened, light golden yellow cheese with mellow to sharp, sometimes smoky, flavor

ragù (rrah-GOO)—thick meat sauce

ravioli (rrahv-YOE-lee)—pasta squares stuffed with cheese, meat, or spinach mixture

ricotta (rree-CAW-tah)—soft, unripened, white cheese with sweet, nutlike flavor; either moist or dry

ripieno (rree-PYAY-no)—stuffing

riso (RREE-zoe)—rice

risotto (rree-ZAW-toe)—rice mixture

salsa (SAHL-sah)—sauce

salsiccia (sahl-SEE-chah)—sausage

scaloppine (skahl-oh-PEE-nay)—thin slices, usually veal

scamorza (skah-MAWRRT-sah)—a light yellow, semisoft cheese with mild flavor

semolino (say-moe-LEE-no)—a coarse meal made from wheat

spaghetti (spah-GHEY-tee)—pasta shaped into long, thin strings; literally "little cords"

spinaci (spee-NAH-chee)—spinach

spumone (spoo-MOE-nay)—an Italian ice cream

tagliatelle (tahl-yah-TEL-lay)—a flat pasta about ¾ inch wide

tartufi (tahrr-TOO-fee)—truffles

torta (TAWRR-tah)—cake, tart, pie

tortellini (tawrr-tay-LEE-nee)—small stuffed pasta rings

tortino (tawrr-TEE-no)—type of omelet

uova (WAW-vah)—eggs

vino (VEE-no)—wine

vitello (vee-TEY-loe)—veal, calf

vongole (VAWN-go-lay)—mussels

zucchini (zoo-KEE-nee)—slender, green, summer squash about 5 inches long

zuppa (ZOO-pah)—soup

Cooking by Regions

VALLE D'AOSTA

Let us enter Italy as Hannibal did—through the Alps. Not to conquer, but rather to capture the true essence of Italian cooking.

A drive southward through the Swiss Alps brings the visitor to Valle d'Aosta, a small area bordering on France and Switzerland, at the top of the Italian boot. The northern backdrop is one of the most imposing to be found anywhere. It is made up of the Matterhorn, Mont Blanc, and Monte Rosa, with peaks vanishing into the clouds.

Valle d'Aosta has an international feeling; French is spoken as readily as Italian. Its people are, for the most part, French in ancestry, and this has influenced the cuisine as much as the language.

At the heart of the region is the city of Aosta itself. It is quite evident that this city dates back to the Romans; it was originally named Augusta Pretoria. It was laid out according to the traditional Roman plan for cities, surrounded by fortress-like walls with towers at each corner that still stand as reminders of that long-ago time.

In the valley are many medieval castles (now hotels) where the local cuisine can be sampled. Mountain trout are as natural in this setting as in the Rockies back home. And as in Switzerland, dairies do well, judging by the success of a local cheese, fontina. It is often served in Fonduta, the Italian version of fondue.

French terms are often found on the menus of the region; beef tournedos, for example, are a specialty. However, cattle raising is an expensive process, and most producers find it more profitable to send the animals to the market young; so veal dishes are more frequently found than beef. One particularly tempting veal dish is Costolette alla Valdostana.

Fruits, especially apples and pears, provide an abundant harvest, but for most of the other fresh produce, the people of Valle d'Aosta must turn to their neighbors.

Veal Cutlets Valle d'Aosta *(Costolette alla Valdostana)*

6 **veal chops, boneless, 1 inch thick**
6 **thin slices fully cooked ham**
6 **slices fontina or mozzarella cheese**
1 **cup all-purpose flour**
1 **teaspoon salt**
¼ **teaspoon pepper**
1 **egg, beaten with 1 tablespoon water**
  Fine bread crumbs
¼ **cup butter, more if needed**

1. Butterfly chops by slicing through the chop almost all the way, and laying chop open so it is ½ inch thick; pound flat.
2. Place a slice of ham, then a slice of cheese, in the center of each chop. Moisten edges of chop and press together.
3. Dip each folded chop first in flour mixed with salt and pepper, then in beaten egg, and finally in the bread crumbs.
4. Heat the butter in a large skillet. Brown the chops slowly, about 5 minutes on each side or until done.

6 servings

Cheese Fondue *(Fonduta)*

Fontina cheese is customarily used in Fonduta, but it is not readily available in the United States. The combination of cheeses makes a good substitute.

1 **pound fontina cheese or ¾ pound mozzarella cheese and ¼ pound Bel Paese**
1 **cup milk**
3 **tablespoons butter**
½ **teaspoon salt**
¼ **teaspoon white pepper**
3 **egg yolks, beaten**
  White truffles, sliced (optional)
1 **loaf (1 pound) Italian or French bread, cut in bite-size pieces**

1. Dice cheese and soak in milk for 30 minutes. Drain.
2. Combine the cheese, butter, salt, and pepper in the top of a chafing dish or double boiler. Place over hot water and heat, stirring steadily, until cheese melts.
3. Very gradually beat in the egg yolks, stirring constantly until thickened. Do not let mixture boil.
4. Serve in the chafing dish, or if prepared in double boiler, pour into a hot serving dish. Sprinkle with truffles, if desired, and surround with pieces of bread. Spear bread with fork and dip.

4 to 6 servings

PIEDMONT

The Piedmont offers a banquet of delights to the sight-seer as well as the diner. It shares borders with Swiss mountain country on the north and with French wine country on the west.

The Piedmont has made some important contributions to culinary culture. One of them is grissini, or breadsticks. Now baked all over the world, they are said to have originated in a Turin bakery. Another is tartufi, light-colored truffles that are found in the Piedmont hills.

Piedmont chefs have been prolific with their inventions. Bollito Misto, the classic Italian boiled dinner, is credited to Piedmont. It is a little like the American boiled dinner, upgraded a notch or two by combining several meats, rather than just one, with a variety of vegetables. Beef is often the basic ingredient. It may be accompanied by chick-en, sausage, pig's feet, and possibly a veal knuckle. At serving time, a sauce is served alongside: either a green or a tomato sauce.

Bagna Cauda, generally credited to the Piedmont, is popular throughout Italy. It is a hot anchovy sauce, heavily laced with garlic, into which strips of fresh vegetables are dipped.

The pasta typical of the Piedmont is agnolotti. This dish bears a resemblance to the ravioli of Genoa, but it also has a personality all its own. Stuffing mixtures for these pastry envelopes run the gamut from meat to vegetables, the ultimate decision depending upon the cook's supplies. In the Piedmontese home at Christmastime, agnolotti are sure to be on the table.

Wine shares equal billing with food in the Piedmont; a good portion of the acreage in the

Alpine foothills is planted in vineyards. Barolo and Barbera are red wines much in demand. The Piedmont also produces Asti Spumante, the sparkling white wine frequently compared with the champagnes of France. Another Piedmont wine known widely, especially to mixers of cocktails, is vermouth.

The Piedmont deserves special attention from historians, wine lovers, and lovers of good food.

Its soul-lifting fare may have been inspired by the same genius that fostered the reunification of Italy in the last century. Victor Emmanuel, headquartered in Turin, sent Garibaldi forth to shape the present-day Italy.

Modern Turin is an industrial city with the Fiat among its better-known products. Visitors are drawn to the Piedmont for its ski resorts, for its beauty, and of course, for its gourmet offerings.

Bagna Cauda

4 stalks celery, cut in 2-inch julienne strips
1 green pepper, cut in strips
2 carrots, pared and cut in 2-inch julienne strips
1 bunch scallions, trimmed
8 cherry tomatoes
1 small head cauliflower, broken into flowerets
8 asparagus spears, trimmed
¼ pound small whole fresh mushrooms
½ cup olive oil
½ cup butter
4 cloves garlic, crushed in a garlic press
8 anchovy fillets, pounded and finely chopped
Freshly ground black pepper
Bread sticks

1. Prepare all vegetables except the mushrooms and place in a bowl of water with ice for 1 hour. Drain vegetables and place on paper towels. Wipe mushrooms with a damp cloth.
2. Arrange the vegetables on a serving tray. Cover tightly with plastic wrap, and refrigerate until ready to serve.
3. Combine olive oil, butter, garlic, and anchovies in a chafing dish or top of a double boiler. Place over simmering water and heat until butter is melted and mixture is thoroughly heated. Sprinkle with a few grains of pepper.
4. Cover and let mixture mellow for 30 minutes. Serve in chafing dish or pour into individual serving dishes and pass the chilled vegetables and bread sticks for dipping.

About 8 servings

Chicken Breasts Regina *(Petti di Pollo Regina)*

2 whole chicken breasts, skinned, boned, and cut in half
4 thin slices ham
4 thin slices liver sausage or liver pâté
Water
Flour
1 egg, beaten
Fine dry bread crumbs
3 tablespoons butter
Madeira Sauce (page 14)

1. Split chicken breast halves lengthwise, but not completely through. Open breast halves and pound until very thin.
2. Place a slice of ham, then a slice of liver sausage in center of each breast. Fold in half, enclosing the ham and liver sausage, moisten the edges with water, and press together.
3. Coat chicken breasts with flour, dip in beaten egg, and coat with bread crumbs.
4. Fry in butter in a skillet until golden brown on both sides. Serve with hot Madeira Sauce.

4 servings

Madeira Sauce

¼ cup chopped celery
¼ cup chopped carrot
2 tablespoons chopped green onion
1 tablespoon cooking oil
1 quart water
2 beef bouillon cubes
1 chicken bouillon cube
½ bay leaf
   Pinch ground thyme
   Few grains freshly ground black
     pepper
1 tablespoon tomato sauce
¼ cup water
2 tablespoons flour
⅓ cup Madeira

1. Cook celery, carrot, and onion in hot oil in a large saucepot until dark brown, but not burned.
2. Stir in 1 quart water, bouillon cubes, bay leaf, thyme, and pepper. Bring to boiling, and simmer until liquid is reduced by half.
3. Strain the liquid. Stir in tomato sauce and bring to boiling.
4. Vigorously shake ¼ cup water and flour in a screw-top jar. While stirring the boiling mixture, slowly add the flour mixture. Cook 1 to 2 minutes, then simmer about 30 minutes, stirring occasionally.
5. Just before serving, stir Madeira into sauce and bring sauce to boiling.

About 2⅓ cups sauce

Bollito Misto

1 fresh beef tongue (3 to 4 pounds)
1 calf's head, prepared for cooking, or 2 pounds veal neck
2 pounds beef (neck, rump, or chuck roast)
2 pig's feet or 1 pound cotechino or other uncooked pork sausage
1 stewing chicken (3 to 4 pounds)
4 medium carrots, pared and cut in 3-inch pieces
2 large stalks celery, cut in pieces
3 onions, peeled and quartered
4 turnips or parsnips, pared and quartered
2 tablespoons chopped parsley
1 teaspoon tarragon
1 teaspoon thyme
   Water
   Salt
   Salsa Verde

1. Combine meats, chicken, vegetables, parsley, tarragon, and thyme in a large sauce pot. Pour in enough water to cover meat, and salt to taste.
2. Cover pot, bring to boiling, and simmer 3 to 4 hours, or until tongue is tender.
3. Remove skin from tongue. Slice meat, cut chicken in serving pieces, and arrange with vegetables on a large platter.
4. Serve with **boiled potatoes, cooked cabbage, beets, pickles,** and Salsa Verde.

10 to 12 servings

Note: A pressure cooker may be used. Follow manufacturer's directions for use of cooker and length of cooking time.

Salsa Verde: Finely chop **3 hard-cooked eggs;** set aside. Combine **½ cup salad oil** and **3 tablespoons wine vinegar.** Add **sugar, salt,** and **pepper** to taste. Mix well and combine with the chopped eggs. Blend in **6 tablespoons chopped herbs** such as **dill, tarragon, chervil, parsley, sorrel,** and **chives.** Refrigerate several hours to allow flavors to blend.

Even the most dedicated gourmet will admit that in Liguria the food must share honors with (if not take a back seat to) the gorgeous scenery. This sun-drenched stretch of the Riviera, crowned with the Alps, needs no other claim to fame.

Despite this fact, Liguria doesn't draw tourists in quite the numbers that flock to its neighbor, the French Riviera. That may be part of its charm. The Italian Riviera has a more straightforward appeal, unburdened with much of the fabrication of tourist havens.

Liguria is an arc along the Mediterranean, so seafood is important in the local cooking. Fishermen at Genoa and other coastal cities fill their nets with red mullet, mackerel, and a host of shellfish, including shrimp. Baby squids (calamaretti) lend adventure to the Ligurian menu, as do bianchetti (very tiny white fish). Mussels are plentiful, and are often served as moules marinière—a verbal reminder, if any is needed, that France is just across the border.

From the hillsides overlooking the ocean come two necessities for the Ligurian cook: olive oil and basil. Olive trees are among the few plants able to survive on the craggy slopes, where even the goats have difficulty maneuvering. The hardy basil manages to hang onto its roothold, too.

Other foods that grow in Liguria are the orange-topped mushroom and chestnuts. The latter are often converted into marrons glacés—another tip of the chef's hat to French influence.

While Ligurian cooking on the whole is not famous, Genoa, foremost city of the region, has provided a cooking style that has earned the highest form of flattery: imitation. "Genovese" in the name of a dish usually indicates a flavor that is subtle, even mild, compared with the more highly seasoned dishes of Naples. Some have described it as "white" compared to the "red" cuisine of the south.

Pesto sauce, attributed to Genoa, is made of chopped leaves of basil, garlic, grated Sardo cheese, pinenuts, and olive oil. It is made by chopping the ingredients, then grinding them with mortar and pestle (which gives name to the sauce). Trenette al pesto is a combination of slender noodles with pesto sauce. Visitors are also likely to encounter gnocchi alla genovese or Gnocchi Verdi on a Ligurian menu. Gnocchi are dumplings made of semolina or potato flour dough, shaped, and either poached or baked.

A few wines are produced in Liguria, but like the local cheeses, are not well known outside Italy. Liguria's greatest feast is the view.

Lasagne with Green Garlic Sauce
(Lasagne al Pesto)

1 pound lasagne noodles
  Green Garlic Sauce (page 16)
1 cup grated Parmesan cheese

1. Cook lasagne noodles according to package directions. Drain. Alternate layers of lasagne, sauce, and cheese in a 2-quart baking dish.
2. Bake at 425°F 15 to 20 minutes, or until hot.

8 to 10 servings

Spaghetti Genoese (Spaghetti alla Genovese)

1 pound long spaghetti
¼ cup olive oil
½ cup butter
2 cloves garlic, finely minced
6 tablespoons chopped parsley
1 pint half-and-half
½ cup grated Parmesan cheese

1. Cook spaghetti according to package directions. Drain.
2. In a large skillet, heat oil and butter over low heat. Add garlic, but do not brown. Stir in parsley and half-and-half; heat slightly, but do not boil.
3. Add spaghetti to cream sauce in skillet; mix well. Blend in cheese, a little at a time, coating all the spaghetti well. Serve on hot plates.

6 to 8 servings

Green Garlic Sauce *(Pesto Genovese)*

3 cloves garlic, peeled
3 tablespoons minced sweet basil
    leaves or 2½ teaspoons dried
    basil leaves
3 tablespoons grated Parmesan or
    Romano cheese
1 tablespoon chopped pinenuts or
    walnuts
¼ teaspoon salt
4 to 6 tablespoons olive oil
1 tablespoon chopped fresh parsley

1. In a mortar, mix garlic, basil, cheese, nuts, and salt. Grind mixture with a pestle to a smooth paste.
2. Still grinding, add very gradually enough olive oil to make a smooth sauce. Stir in parsley.
3. To serve, add desired amount of sauce and a tablespoon of butter to hot pasta and mix well at the table. Accompany with grated cheese, if desired.

About ½ cup sauce

Note: Sauce may be stored in refrigerator with a little olive oil on top.

Cheese-Spinach Gnocchi *(Gnocchi Verdi)*

1½ cups milk
1 tablespoon butter
¼ teaspoon salt
    Few grains ground nutmeg
¼ cup uncooked farina
½ cup well-drained cooked
    chopped spinach
1 egg, well beaten
1 tablespoon chopped onion,
    lightly browned in 1 teaspoon
    butter
1½ cups shredded Swiss cheese
2 eggs, well beaten
¾ cup milk
1 tablespoon flour
1 teaspoon salt
    Few grains ground nutmeg

1. Bring milk, butter, salt, and nutmeg to boiling in a saucepan. Add farina gradually, stirring constantly over low heat until mixture thickens.
2. Stir in spinach, egg, onion, and 1 cup shredded cheese; mix well. Remove from heat and set aside to cool slightly.
3. Drop mixture by tablespoonfuls close together in a well-greased 9-inch shallow baking pan or casserole. Sprinkle mounds with remaining cheese.
4. Combine remaining ingredients and pour over spinach mounds.
5. Bake at 350°F 35 to 40 minutes, or until topping is golden brown.

About 6 servings

Baked Shrimp *(Scampi al Forno)*

2 pounds large fresh uncooked
    shrimp
⅓ cup butter
1 teaspoon salt
4 cloves garlic, crushed in a garlic
    press
¼ cup chopped parsley
2 teaspoons grated lemon peel
2 tablespoons lemon juice

1. Remove shells from shrimp, leaving shell on tail section. Remove vein down the back, wash under cold running water, and drain on paper towels.
2. Place butter in a 13×9-inch baking dish; heat in oven at 400°F until melted. Stir in salt, garlic, and 1 tablespoon parsley. Place shrimp in a single layer in the baking dish.
3. Bake at 400°F 5 minutes. Turn the shrimp and sprinkle with lemon peel, lemon juice, and remaining parsley. Continue baking about 15 minutes, or until tender.
4. Serve shrimp with sauce over **hot fluffy rice.**

About 6 servings

Typical ingredients and equipment from the regions

The American planning his first visit to Italy might overlook Lombardy; Rome, Venice, and other attractions are better known to him. Yet he could be missing some rare experiences, both visual and victual.

Milan, at the heart of Lombardy, has been called Italy's most opulent city, and it has a cuisine to match. The classic rice dish, Risotto alla Milanese, offers saffron-tinted elegance. Minestrone is claimed by other regions, but the Milanese defend their title as originators of the first and best.

In Milan, Ossobuco is often served with gremolada sauce, a harmony of lemon, garlic, rosemary, parsley, and sage. Panettone is a large, slightly sweet bread, with flecks of colorful candied fruit peel and raisins. Rarely made at home any more, Pannetone is featured by bakeries at Christmastime.

Of course, Milan boasts leadership in other fields as well. La Scala has attracted the finest of operatic talent for centuries. Leonardo da Vinci completed "The Last Supper" in Milan—shortly before Columbus left for the Orient by way of the New World. Paintings by Bellini, Raphael, and other giants of the art world hang in Milan.

Milan's greatest architectural achievement is the cathedral; its square is a favorite meeting place.

The visitor who ventures outside Milan will be rewarded, too. The cheeses of Lombardy have won far more than local fame. Perhaps the best known is Gorgonzola, the blue-veined variety that is somewhat like Roquefort. The famous Bel Paese originated in Lombardy, but is now duplicated in other regions, and even in other countries. Fior d'Alpe (flower of the Alps) is similar, and comes from the town of Lodi. Several good cream cheeses are made in Lombardy.

While the wines of Lombardy are not up to its cheeses, a few agreeable vintages come from the area around Lake Garda. The lakes themselves are more productive, supporting a flourishing fishing industry. The trout is particularly prized. While not as elegant, little sardines called agoni provide the major catch.

Meatballs are a relative rarity in Italy. This may come as a surprise to Americans accustomed to serving them at home with spaghetti. Yet there is a version made in Lombardy called Polpette. These are flavored with lemon zest, nutmeg, and herbs. Like the other recipes of Lombardy, it is well worth an acquaintance.

Ossobuco

4 to 5 pounds veal shank crosscuts
 Flour
⅓ cup olive oil
 Salt and pepper
½ cup beef broth or bouillon
1 onion, chopped
1 clove garlic, crushed in a garlic
 press
1 medium carrot, sliced
1 leek, sliced
1 slice celery root
2 whole cloves
1 bay leaf
 Pinch each of sage, thyme, and
 rosemary
½ cup white wine
1 can (28 ounces) whole tomatoes
1 tablespoon grated lemon peel

1. Dredge crosscuts with flour. Heat several tablespoons olive oil in a skillet. Brown the veal well, season with salt and pepper, and transfer to a heatproof casserole or Dutch oven. Handle gently so the marrow remains in the bones. Pour the broth into the casserole.

2. Add more oil to skillet, if needed. In hot oil, sauté onion, garlic, carrot, leek, and celery root over medium heat about 5 minutes.

3. Stir in the cloves, bay leaf, sage, thyme, and rosemary. Pour in the wine and continue cooking until wine is almost evaporated. Stir in tomatoes and grated lemon peel. Cook over medium heat several minutes.

4. Pour tomato mixture over meat in casserole. Cover tightly and simmer about 1½ hours, or until meat is tender. Remove veal to serving dish and keep hot.

5. Force vegetables and juice in casserole through a sieve or food mill. If the resulting sauce is thin, cook over high heat to reduce liquid. Season sauce, if necessary. Pour sauce over meat or serve separately.

6. Serve with **rice** or **spaghetti** tossed with **melted butter** and topped with **grated Parmesan** or **Romano cheese**.

4 or 5 servings

Minestrone, 18, from Lombardy

Minestrone

Derived from the Latin "to hand out," this soup was a staple in the days when the monks kept it always on the fire to be ready for sojourners or travelers. Even today, it is a favorite.

6 cups water
1¼ cups (about ½ pound) dried navy beans, rinsed
¼ pound salt pork
3 tablespoons olive oil
1 small onion, chopped
1 clove garlic, chopped
¼ head cabbage
2 stalks celery, cut in ½-inch slices
2 small carrots, pared and cut in ½-inch slices
1 medium potato, pared and diced
1 tablespoon chopped parsley
½ teaspoon salt
¼ teaspoon pepper
1 quart hot water
¼ cup packaged precooked rice
½ cup frozen green peas
¼ cup tomato paste
Grated Parmesan cheese

1. Bring the 6 cups water to boiling in a large saucepot. Gradually add the beans to the boiling water so the boiling does not stop. Simmer the beans 2 minutes, and remove from heat. Set aside to soak 1 hour.
2. Add salt pork to beans and return to heat. Bring to boiling, reduce heat, and simmer 1 hour, stirring once or twice.
3. While beans are simmering with salt pork, heat the olive oil in a skillet, and brown the onion and garlic lightly. Set aside.
4. Wash the cabbage, discarding coarse outer leaves, and shred finely.
5. After the beans have simmered an hour, add the onion, garlic, celery, carrots, potato, cabbage, parsley, salt, and pepper. Slowly pour in 1 quart hot water and simmer about 1 hour, or until the beans are tender.
6. Meanwhile, cook the rice according to package directions. About 10 minutes before the beans should be done, stir in the rice and peas. When the peas are tender, stir in the tomato paste. Simmer about 5 minutes. Serve sprinkled with cheese.

About 6 servings

Meatballs *(Polpette)*

Peel of 1 lemon, grated
1 sprig parsley
2 cloves garlic, peeled
1 pound ground beef
1 teaspoon salt
¼ teaspoon pepper
Pinch grated nutmeg
1 slice bread, crumbled
Milk
1 egg, beaten
2 to 3 tablespoons olive oil or other cooking oil

1. Mince together grated lemon peel, parsley, and garlic.
2. Mix ground beef with salt, pepper, nutmeg, and lemon-peel mixture.
3. Soak bread in a small amount of milk, squeeze dry, and add with egg to meat mixture. Blend well.
4. On a lightly floured surface, form mixture into patties about ½ inch thick and 1½ inches wide.
5. Place the patties in hot oil in a skillet. Brown about 2 minutes on each side. Drain and serve hot.

4 to 6 servings

Braised Rice with Saffron *(Risotto alla Milanese)*

¼ cup butter
¼ cup finely chopped onion
1 cup uncooked rice
3 cups chicken broth
½ cup Marsala

1. Melt butter in a heavy 1½-quart saucepan with a tight-fitting cover. Add onion and cook until lightly browned. Stir in uncooked rice. Cook slowly until rice is lightly browned, stirring occasionally with a fork.
2. Slowly stir in broth, wine, and salt. Place over high heat

1 teaspoon salt
¼ teaspoon saffron
2 tablespoons hot water
¼ cup grated Parmesan cheese

and stir with a fork until mixture boils. Cover pan, reduce heat, and allow rice to simmer without stirring 18 minutes.

3. Turn off heat, leave pan in place, and keep on cover to allow rice to steam. While rice is steaming, dissolve saffron in hot water.

4. After 30 minutes, the rice should absorb all the liquid and be tender, fluffy, and dry. Add saffron mixture to rice and mix well, using a fork to lift and turn the rice.

5. Serve rice warm, topped with cheese.

4 or 5 servings

Fruit Bread, Milan Style (Panettone)

The traditional Christmas bread of Italy.

2 packages active dry yeast
¼ cup warm water
1 cup butter, melted
1 cup sugar
1 teaspoon salt
2 cups sifted all-purpose flour
½ cup milk, scalded and cooled to
    lukewarm
2 eggs
4 egg yolks
3½ cups all-purpose flour
1 cup dark seedless raisins
¾ cup chopped citron
½ cup all-purpose flour
1 egg, slightly beaten
1 tablespoon water

1. Dissolve yeast in the warm water.

2. Pour melted butter into large bowl of electric mixer. Add the sugar and salt gradually, beating constantly.

3. Beating thoroughly after each addition, alternately add the 2 cups flour in thirds and lukewarm milk in halves to the butter mixture. Add yeast and beat well.

4. Combine eggs and egg yolks and beat until thick and piled softly. Add the beaten eggs all at one time to yeast mixture and beat well. Beating thoroughly after each addition, gradually add the 3½ cups flour. Stir in raisins and citron.

5. Sift half of the remaining ½ cup flour over a pastry canvas or board. Turn dough onto floured surface; cover and let rest 10 minutes.

6. Sift remaining flour over dough. Pull dough from edges toward center until flour is worked in. (It will be sticky.) Put dough into a greased deep bowl and grease top of dough. Cover; let rise in a warm place (about 80°F) about 2½ hours.

7. Punch down dough and pull edges of dough in to center. Let rise again about 1 hour.

8. Divide dough into halves and shape each into a round loaf. Put each loaf into a well-greased 8-inch layer cake pan. Brush surfaces generously with a mixture of slightly beaten egg and water. Cover; let rise again about 1 hour.

9. Bake at 350°F 40 to 45 minutes, or until golden brown. Remove to wire racks to cool.

2 panettoni

TRENTINO-ALTO ADIGE

The cooking of Trentino-Alto Adige is, like the name, a mixture. Since it was once part of the Austrian Tyrol, the cultural heritage is hybrid. The language spoken is often German; the architecture, Tyrolean. Tyrolean and Italian cooking marry harmoniously in the region; the restaurant menus are often printed in both languages. Ravioli is popular, but so is sauerkraut, served with an array of sausages and smoked pork. And beer often accompanies meals, in the Teutonic style.

Polenta is popular in Trentino-Alto Adige, but the local version uses saraceno grain, rather than the cornmeal that is more usual. Gnocchi is seen in a different form here, too; smoked pork and parsley are added to the usual ingredients, and they are served with sauerkraut. Rabbit is abundantly available from the woods, and one should not be surprised to find hasenpfeffer!

Residents of Trentino-Alto Adige have a fondness for pastry, and local shops offer displays of baked goods from both Italy and Germany. Orecchie di lepre, meaning "rabbit's ear," is a delicate little cake in the shape of a rabbit's ear. Strudel, likewise, is in demand.

Trentino-Alto Adige is fruit-growing country. The valleys are fertile and blessed with rainfall bounteous enough to nurture fruit and vegetable fields. Grapes thrive, too. While the local vintages are not as well known as those from neighboring regions, wines from Riesling, Sylvaner, Sauvignon, and Pinot grapes all make pleasant partners for the food of the region. And all are from Germany or France, completing the picture of crossbred cuisine.

Along with two neighboring regions, Trentino-Alto Adige belongs to an area known as Venetia, perhaps a nod to the preeminence of the city Venice as its brightest light. Its borders have shifted with the settlement of every major war. Trentino-Alto Adige owes its present outline to the Treaty of Versailles in 1919.

But the cultural mix gives the tourist a feeling of enjoying two countries at once; the magnificent Dolomites add a bonus to the bargain.

Soup Dumplings *(Canederli)*

1 slice bacon, diced
1 teaspoon butter
½ cup minced onion
½ cup peeled fresh Italian sausage, cut in small pieces
2½ cups coarsely crumbled dry bread
1 cup milk
3 eggs
1 tablespoon minced parsley
2 tablespoons grated Parmesan cheese
Dash nutmeg
½ teaspoon salt
Dash pepper
2 cups all-purpose flour
2 quarts chicken consommé or broth, boiling

1. Place bacon, butter, onion, and sausage in saucepan. Cook until onion is soft. Mix in bread and cook 1 or 2 minutes.
2. Remove mixture from heat and stir in milk. Set aside for at least 1 hour.
3. Add eggs, one at a time, mixing well after each is added. Stir in parsley, cheese, nutmeg, salt, and pepper. Add the flour, stirring until mixture holds together.
4. Form mixture into balls no larger than a walnut, and drop, one at a time, into the boiling consommé in a large pot. Reduce heat and allow dumplings to cook 20 to 25 minutes.
5. Serve broth and dumplings, sprinkled with grated Parmesan cheese.

6 to 8 servings

Note: If desired, dumplings may be cooked in boiling salted water, drained, and served with melted butter or a meat sauce.

Viennese Fried Cakes *(Faschingskrapfen)*

½ envelope active dry yeast
⅓ cup warm water
¼ teaspoon salt
1½ teaspoons sugar
1 cup half-and-half (at room temperature)
3½ tablespoons melted butter
3 egg yolks, lightly beaten
3 cups all-purpose flour
Maraschino cherries or apricot jam
Milk
Clarified butter or butter and lard
Confectioners' sugar

1. Dissolve yeast in warm water. Stir in salt, sugar, half-and-half, melted butter, and egg yolks. Stir in 2 cups flour, and add enough additional flour to form a soft but manageable dough.
2. Knead the dough briefly, place in a floured bowl, and cover with a cloth. Let rise in a warm place until doubled in bulk (about 1 hour).
3. Knead dough down lightly and turn onto a floured board. Pull or roll the dough gently until it is ¼ inch thick. Cut dough into 2-inch rounds, using a biscuit cutter.
4. In the centers of half the rounds, place a maraschino cherry or 1 teaspoon apricot jam. Brush these rounds with milk and cover with remaining rounds, pressing the edges together very lightly.
5. Place the filled rounds on a floured baking sheet or towel and let stand for 30 minutes in a warm place.
6. Fry them a few at a time in hot butter 2 inches deep in a saucepan. Do not crowd. After placing in hot butter, cover the pan for a minute or two; then turn the cakes. When they are golden, remove from butter, and drain on paper towels.
7. Sprinkle generously with confectioners' sugar and serve.

20 cakes

Widows' Kisses *(Witwe Küsse)*

4 egg whites
½ cup plus 2 tablespoons granulated sugar
1 cup chopped nuts (almonds or walnuts)
¼ cup finely diced citron

1. In the top of a double boiler set over simmering water, beat egg whites with the sugar. Use a rotary beater and beat the mixture until it is fairly stiff.
2. Remove the top of double boiler from hot water and stir in nuts and citron. Drop by level tablespoons about 1 inch apart onto greased baking sheets.
3. Bake at 300°F 25 to 30 minutes. Cookies should be just lightly browned. Leave on baking sheet 1 to 2 minutes before removing to cooling rack.

About 3½ dozen cookies

VENETO EUGANEA

While the name "Veneto" (or Venetia) is hardly a household term for most Americans, the name of its leading city, Venice, needs no introduction. Both in history and literature, Venice has been immortalized.

The traveler to Venice is first drawn to the Piazza San Marco, the museums filled with great paintings, and to the canals for a ride in a gondola. After such exalting experiences, he is ready for the ultimate in dining, and he will not be disappointed.

The region of Veneto and the city of Venice itself are located on the Adriatic Sea, so it follows that seafood is an important part of the daily fare. Venice was once a bustling seaport, the destination of trading ships from the Orient. Spices delivered to Venice were the cornerstone of trade for the early Romans, and spices are still important in the Venetian kitchen. Seafood en papillote is a combination of the local fish with the wizardry of clever seasoning; the name is borrowed from the French. Fish soup, or Zuppa di Pesce, is often prepared. So is the Venetian risotto, laden with scampi or mussels.

Even those Venetian visitors who claim to dislike liver have been won over by fegato alla veneziana. Onions, lemon juice, wine, and an artful touch of seasonings work magic.

Venetians are credited with inventing Risi e Bisi, rice and peas cooked together. Another combination created locally is pasta e fagioli, macaroni cooked with beans. This combination is a hearty appetite satisfier, and is nutritious enough to stand as a complete meal on its own.

Polenta, popular everywhere in Italy, is a special favorite in Veneto. Italy has a way of transforming all who visit, and evidently this applies even to food. Cornmeal was introduced from the New World, but went back home with a whole new personality, served as polenta.

Cornmeal is used to good advantage also in the patty-cakes of Venice, suitable for a family meal. Big desserts aren't customary; simple desserts such as fresh fruit are more common throughout Italy. However, the special-occasion meal is something else; then look for something as mouth-watering as chocolate gâteau.

Outside Venice, it is in the wine department that Veneto really shines. Valpolicella, made in the neighborhood of Verona, is outstanding among its reds. It ages well and develops into a perfect partner for roasts and game. Bardolino is another well-known wine; it is sometimes compared to Chianti. Veneto is the home of a famous white wine, too, called Soave. It is pronounced "suave" and has a polish to match; it pairs well with fish.

Venice may be first for the tourist's money, but there are other cities in the region with interesting histories and visual treasures for the visitor. Scenically, the Dolomites and Lake Garda are major attractions.

Zuppa di Pesce: Royal Danieli

This fish soup recipe is from the Danieli Royal Excelsior, a hotel in Venice.

   3 **pounds skinned and boned fish (haddock, trout, cod, salmon, and red snapper)**
   1 **lobster (about 1 pound)**
   1 **pound shrimp with shells**
   1 **quart water**
   ½ **cup coarsely cut onion**
   1 **stalk celery with leaves, coarsely cut**
   2 **tablespoons cider vinegar**
   2 **teaspoons salt**
   ¼ **cup olive oil**
   2 **cloves garlic, minced**
   1 **bay leaf, crumbled**
   1 **teaspoon basil**
   ½ **teaspoon thyme**
   2 **tablespoons minced parsley**
   ½ **to 1 cup dry white wine**
   ½ **cup chopped peeled tomatoes**
   8 **shreds saffron**
   1 **teaspoon salt**
   ½ **teaspoon freshly ground black pepper**
   6 **slices French bread**
   ¼ **cup olive oil**

1. Reserve heads and tails of fish. Cut fish into bite-size pieces.
2. In a saucepot or kettle, boil lobster and shrimp 5 minutes in water with onion, celery, vinegar, and 2 teaspoons salt.
3. Remove and shell lobster and shrimp; devein shrimp. Cut lobster into bite-size pieces. Set lobster and shrimp aside.
4. Return shells to the broth and add heads and tails of fish. Simmer 20 minutes.
5. Strain broth, pour into saucepot, and set aside.
6. Sauté all of the fish in ¼ cup oil with garlic, bay leaf, basil, thyme, and parsley 5 minutes, stirring constantly.
7. Add to reserved broth along with wine, tomatoes, saffron, 1 teaspoon salt, and the pepper. Bring to boiling; cover and simmer 10 minutes, stirring occasionally.
8. Serve with slices of bread sautéed in the remaining ¼ cup olive oil.

About 2½ quarts soup

Venetian Rice and Peas *(Risi e Bisi)*

3 tablespoons olive oil
3 tablespoons unsalted butter
2 slices prosciutto, cut in pieces
1 small onion, minced
3 tablespoons chopped parsley
1 package (10 ounces) frozen green
    peas (or 1 pound fresh)
  Water
1 cup uncooked rice, long or short
    grain
1 quart chicken broth
  Grated Parmesan cheese

1. Put oil and butter into a large saucepan over medium heat. Add prosciutto, onion, and parsley. Sauté until onion is translucent. Add peas and enough water to cover (about ½ inch), and cook 5 minutes.
2. Stir in rice and chicken broth; bring to a boil. Reduce heat and simmer about 15 minutes, stirring frequently, or until the rice is tender.
3. Serve with Parmesan cheese.

6 to 8 servings

Polenta

3 cups water
2 chicken bouillon cubes
1 cup yellow cornmeal
2 tablespoons butter or margarine

1. Bring water to boiling. Stir in bouillon cubes to dissolve. Slowly stir in cornmeal. Reduce heat and cook, stirring, until very thick (about 7 minutes).
2. Remove from heat and stir in butter until melted.
3. Spoon onto plates and top each serving with 1 tablespoon butter or 2 tablespoons shredded mozzarella, Monterey Jack, or Cheddar cheese. Serve as a meat accompaniment.

4 servings

 **FRIULI-VENEZIA GIULIA**

The "Friuli" in the name of this region recalls the Roman Forum, and "Giulia," the emperor Julius. That's a fair clue to the age of this area. While it can't compete with neighboring Venice for travel inducements, it has a history that is equally rich, along with sights and savory food to delight the visitor.

After World War II, Italy lost a portion of this region, but picked up Trieste from Yugoslavia. The population, and therefore the language and the cooking, is a mélange of Austrian, Hungarian, and Slavic as well as Italian. Costoletta alla Viennese, a dish that is popular in the region, is simply wiener schnitzel in Italian dress. The Hungarian national dish, gulyas, is also served in Friuli-Venezia Giulia, but veal or pork substitute for the more familiar beef of the original.

Trieste is famous for its soup. A hearty chowder concocted of beans, potatoes, and sauerkraut, boiled with pork and laced with garlic, is called iola Triestina. Various forms of fish soup also are available in this Adriatic port region.

Udine is a pleasant way station on the road between Venice and Vienna. For a relatively little-known city, it fairly bursts with impressive buildings, some in the "wedding cake" style sometimes seen in Italian architecture. A dinner in Udine might include a selection of ham, seafood, and veal dishes on the menu, served with minestrone and some form of polenta. Pastries are available, but an Italian meal often concludes with a simpler offering of fruit and cheese.

Shrimp San Giusto (Scampi Imperiali San Giusto)

1 pound large uncooked shrimp
½ teaspoon salt
⅛ teaspoon pepper
1 bay leaf
3 tablespoons lemon juice
2½ cups water
1 bay leaf
1 thick slice onion
  Pinch each salt, pepper, thyme, and oregano
2 tablespoons olive oil
1 tablespoon butter
½ cup finely chopped onion
1 clove garlic, finely chopped
1 teaspoon finely chopped parsley
  Flour
⅓ cup dry white wine
1 large tomato, peeled, seeded, and chopped

1. Using scissors, cut the shells of the shrimp down middle of back; remove shells and set aside. Clean and devein shrimp.
2. Place cleaned shrimp in a bowl with salt, pepper, and a bay leaf; drizzle with lemon juice. Set shrimp aside to marinate 1 hour.
3. To make fish stock, place shrimp shells in a saucepan with water, a bay leaf, onion slice, salt, pepper, thyme, and oregano. Cover and simmer 30 minutes; strain.
4. Heat olive oil and butter in a skillet. Add chopped onion, garlic, and parsley; cook until soft. Coat marinated shrimp with flour, add to skillet with vegetables, and cook until lightly browned on both sides.
5. Add wine and simmer until it is almost evaporated. Stir in tomato and ½ cup or more of the strained fish stock. Simmer 15 to 20 minutes, or until the sauce is desired consistency.

3 or 4 servings

Polenta with Sausage (Polenta con Salsiccia)

1 pound Italian sausage
2 tablespoons olive oil
1 pound mushrooms, cleaned and sliced
2½ cups canned tomatoes
1 teaspoon salt
¼ teaspoon pepper
3 cups water
1½ teaspoons salt
1 cup yellow cornmeal
1 cup cold water
  Grated Parmesan or Romano cheese

1. Cut sausage casing, remove sausage, and crumble into small pieces with a fork.
2. Heat olive oil in large skillet. Add sausage and mushrooms to skillet. Cook slowly, stirring occasionally, until the mushrooms and sausage are lightly browned.
3. Slowly stir in the tomatoes, 1 teaspoon salt, and pepper. Simmer 20 to 30 minutes.
4. While the tomato and sausage mixture is simmering, bring 3 cups water with 1½ teaspoons salt to boiling. Gradually stir in the cornmeal and 1 cup cold water. Continue boiling, stirring constantly, until the mixture is thickened.
5. Cover, lower the heat, and cook slowly 10 minutes or longer, if necessary. Transfer the cooked cornmeal to warm platter, and top with the tomato mixture.
6. Sprinkle with cheese and serve immediately.

6 to 8 servings

EMILIA-ROMAGNA

In the region of Emilia-Romagna are two cities with strong food associations: Bologna and Parma. Their names have been attached to a couple of items that are everyday fare in this country—bologna sausage and Parmesan cheese.

But a closer look gives far more insight into the cuisine of Emilia-Romagna. The northernmost part of this region has been compared to the farm belt of the midwestern United States. The fresh produce and pork from its farms provide the makings for Emilia-Romagna's many-splendored dishes.

Emilia-Romagna covers almost the entire width of Italy, sharing its western border with the Mediterranean-coastal province of Liguria, and extending in the east to the Adriatic shore. In the east-coast port of Rimini stands the ancient Arch of Augustus. The arch was built where two famous Roman roads meet, the Via Flaminia and the Via Emilia, which latter lends its name to the region. In Rimini one expects to find excellent seafood dishes, and is not disappointed.

Taking the Via Emilia inland leads to Bologna, the capital city. The American newcomer will probably seek out its sausage, but may be surprised to find that the authentic version is a far cry from the "baloney" he knows. Mortadella is a savory blend of chopped pork and seasonings. The local customers find the salami of Parma and the zampone of Modena just as appealing.

A better acquaintance with the region shows that its cooking style is most notable for its pasta creations. Sfoglia is the foundation for many of them. Sfoglia is a word meaning "leaf," as does the Greek phyllo, and it is as important to the Italian cooking as phyllo is to Greek. From it come such creations as tortellini, cappelletti, and lasagne.

The tortellini are made by rolling sfoglia around a seasoned meat and cheese stuffing. Cappelletti, or "little caps," are similar, but fashioned into a hat shape. Lasagne needs no introduction to the American diner, but in Emilia-Romagna it is sometimes tinted green through the addition of spinach to the dough.

Cheeses are given special attention in Emilia-Romagna, and the one that bears Parma's name is incorporated into a multitude of pasta and meat dishes. "Parmagiana" on the Italian menu is the clue that this full-flavored cheese is among the ingredients of the particular dish.

Wines from Emilia-Romagna are locally popular but only a few, such as Lambrusco, are known outside the country.

A drive through the Apennine foothills is an outstanding part of any visit to Emilia-Romagna; the medieval hostelries along the way are known for their food.

"Little Hats" in Broth (Cappelletti in Brodo)

½ cup (4 ounces) ricotta or cottage cheese
2 tablespoons grated Parmesan cheese
½ cup finely chopped cooked chicken
1 egg, slightly beaten
⅛ teaspoon salt
  Few grains nutmeg
  Few grains pepper
2 cups sifted all-purpose flour
¼ teaspoon salt
2 eggs
3 tablespoons cold water
2 quarts chicken broth or bouillon

1. Combine cheeses, chicken, 1 egg, ⅛ teaspoon salt, nutmeg, and pepper; set aside.
2. Combine flour and ¼ teaspoon salt in a large bowl. Make a well in the center of the flour. Place 2 eggs, one at a time, in the well, mixing slightly after each one is added. Gradually add the water; mix well to make a stiff dough. Turn dough onto a lightly floured surface and knead until smooth and elastic (5 to 8 minutes).
3. Roll dough out to about ¹⁄₁₆ inch thick. Cut into 2½-inch circles. Place ½ teaspoon of the chicken-cheese mixture in the center of each round. Dampen the edges with water, fold in half, and press together to seal. Bring the two ends together, dampen, and pinch together.
4. Bring the chicken broth to boiling. Add pasta and cook 20 to 25 minutes, or until pasta is tender. Pour broth and pasta into soup bowls, and serve immediately.

8 servings

Baked Green Lasagne Bolognese
(Lasagne Verdi al Forno Bolognese)

6 quarts water
1 teaspoon salt
¾ pound Green Lasagne (page 27)
2½ cups Bolognese Meat Sauce
    (page 85)
2 cups Cream Sauce
¾ cup grated Parmesan cheese

1. Bring water to boiling in a large saucepot. Add salt and cook lasagne strips a few at a time for 3 minutes. Remove from boiling water with a strainer, and drop into cold water. Drain again and spread on damp towels.
2. Cover the bottom of a buttered 2-quart baking dish with meat sauce, a small amount of Cream Sauce, and a sprinkling of cheese. Next form a layer of noodles with the ends turning part way up at the sides of the dish. Repeat layering with meat sauce, Cream Sauce, cheese, and lasagne, forming about 6 layers. Finish top with meat sauce, Cream Sauce, and a generous amount of cheese.
3. Bake at 375°F 20 to 25 minutes, or until hot and bubbly.

6 servings

Cream Sauce: Melt **2 tablespoons butter** in a saucepan and blend with **2 tablespoons flour**. Gradually stir in **1 cup milk** and **1 cup half-and-half**. Season with **½ teaspoon salt** and a **dash nutmeg**. Cook, stirring constantly, until sauce boils and thickens. Cover with a sheet of waxed paper on surface and keep warm until ready to use.

2 cups sauce

Rice Cake (Torta de Riso)

3 cups milk
¼ cup uncooked long grain white
    rice
½ cup sugar
¼ teaspoon salt
2 tablespoons butter
1 cup all-purpose flour
2 tablespoons sugar
6 tablespoons firm butter
1 egg yolk, beaten
½ cup chopped blanched almonds
3 eggs, beaten
¼ teaspoon almond extract

1. Combine milk, rice, ½ cup sugar, salt, and 2 tablespoons butter in the top of a double boiler. Set over simmering water, cover, and cook 2¼ to 2½ hours, or until rice is soft; stir occasionally.
2. While the rice is cooking, prepare the pastry. Combine flour, 2 tablespoons sugar, and 6 tablespoons butter. Rub mixture between fingers until butter is the size of rolled oats. Stir in egg yolk and work dough until it forms a ball. Press dough onto bottom and sides of a 9-inch layer cake pan with removable bottom.
3. Bake pastry at 325°F 30 minutes, or until lightly browned. Cool on a wire rack. Place almonds in a shallow pan. Bake at 325°F 15 minutes, or until golden; stir occasionally.
4. Stir some of the hot cooked rice mixture into the beaten eggs. Immediately stir back into mixture in double boiler. Stir in almonds and almond extract, and pour filling into baked pastry crust.
5. Bake at 400°F 20 minutes, or until center is set. Remove pan sides, leaving cake on pan bottom. Serve warm or cool, cut in wedges.

About 8 servings

Cauliflower à la Romagna
(Cavolfiore alla Romagna)

1 head cauliflower, washed and
    trimmed
⅔ cup fine dry bread crumbs
1 teaspoon grated Parmesan cheese
½ teaspoon salt
¼ teaspoon pepper
2 eggs, slightly beaten
¼ cup milk
    Fat for deep frying heated to
    365°F

1. Put whole cauliflower into a saucepan containing a 1-inch depth of boiling salted water. Cook, uncovered, 5 minutes. Cover and cook 15 to 20 minutes, or until cauliflower is tender. Drain, separate into flowerets, and set aside to cool.
2. Combine crumbs, cheese, salt, and pepper. Mix eggs and milk in a small bowl. Coat flowerets with egg mixture, then with crumbs.
3. Put only as many flowerets into fat at one time as will float uncrowded. Fry 2 to 4 minutes, or until golden brown; turn occasionally during frying.
4. Drain and serve hot.

About 4 servings

Green Lasagne (Lasagne Verdi)

½ pound spinach
4 cups all-purpose flour
1 teaspoon salt
2 large eggs, beaten

1. Wash spinach and place in heavy saucepan. Do not add water; cook only in moisture remaining on leaves from washing. Partially cover and cook 5 minutes, stirring occasionally with a fork.
2. Drain spinach, press out the water, chop it, and force it through a sieve; or drain, press out water, and purée in an electric blender. It should retain its fresh green color and become a smooth purée. If the purée is very wet, heat it in the saucepan, about a minute, over very high heat to evaporate some of the moisture. Allow it to cool.
3. Sift the flour and salt into a large mixing bowl. Make a well in the center of the flour and put the beaten eggs and puréed spinach in it. Mix gradually with one hand, or with a fork, until the paste is well blended. If the mixture is too dry, add some water until it forms a ball. If the dough is too sticky, add more flour.
4. Knead the dough at least 12 minutes, until it is smooth and elastic. Divide dough in 4 pieces and roll out to ¹⁄₁₆-inch thick. Cut the sheets of dough into 4×2-inch rectangles, or longer, if desired. The dough may also be cut in squares. Let cut pieces of dough dry on towels for an hour. If not using immediately, store at room temperature.

About 1¼ pounds pasta

Green Noodles: Follow recipe for Green Lasagne. Roll the sheets of dough up and cut in ¼-inch-wide strips. Unroll and place on towels for half an hour to dry. Place in **boiling salted water** and cook 5 minutes; drain. Serve tossed with **butter** and **grated cheese,** or any sauce desired.

Stuffed Pasta Rings in Cream
(Tortellini alla Bolognese)

½ turkey breast (about 2½ pounds), boned
4 slices prosciutto
1 medium-size veal sweetbread, blanched and cleaned
¼ pound lean pork
¼ pound lean beef
7 tablespoons butter
¼ pound Parmesan cheese, grated
2 egg yolks, beaten
Pinch grated nutmeg
Pinch ground cinnamon
Salt and pepper
Pasta Dough for Tortellini
4 quarts chicken broth
1 cup whipping cream

1. Cut turkey breast, prosciutto, sweetbread, pork, and beef into pieces.
2. Melt 4 tablespoons of the butter in a large skillet. Sauté meats until sweetbread pieces are cooked. Remove from heat and cool.
3. Put meat mixture through a meat grinder twice, so it is very finely ground. Place the ground meat in a large bowl and stir in half the cheese, the egg yolks, nutmeg, cinnamon, and salt and pepper to taste. Blend well.
4. Prepare Pasta Dough for Tortellini, using turkey mixture for filling. Set aside on a cloth, cover with another cloth, and allow to dry 30 minutes.
5. Bring the chicken broth to a gentle simmer, not a violent boil or the pasta will break apart. Melt the remaining 3 tablespoons butter in a large saucepot over low heat.
6. Carefully drop filled tortellini, a few at a time, into the gently simmering broth. Simmer until cooked through, but still a little firm (about 10 minutes). Remove, using a slotted spoon, and place in melted butter in saucepot. When all the tortellini are cooked and in the saucepot, pour in the whipping cream and sprinkle remaining cheese over tortellini. Stir gently with a wooden spoon until sauce is smooth.
7. Serve immediately in heated soup bowls. Accompany with additional grated Parmesan cheese.

About 8 servings

Note: A 2-pound frozen boneless turkey roast (thawed) may be substituted for the turkey breast.

Pasta Dough for Tortellini

3½ cups all-purpose flour
1 teaspoon salt
2 eggs, beaten
1 tablespoon olive oil
Warm water (about ½ cup)

1. Put flour on a board and sprinkle with salt. Make a well and add eggs and oil. Mix well until a soft smooth dough is formed. Add warm water gradually, if necessary, to soften dough. Knead 5 to 10 minutes until dough is smooth and elastic. Cover with a bowl for 30 minutes.
2. Divide dough in quarters. Roll each quarter into a round as thin as possible. Cut into 2-inch rounds.
3. For each tortellini, place ¼ to ½ teaspoon filling in center of round. Moisten edges with water. Fold in half; seal edges. Shape into rings by stretching the tips of half circle slightly and wrapping the ring around your index finger. Gently press tips together.
4. Cook as directed.

About 12 dozen tortellini

TUSCANY

The name Tuscany is an indication of the age of this region. It comes from "Etruscan," the name of the people who lived there almost a thousand years before the time of Christ.

With a heritage of so many centuries, the culture and cooking of Tuscany have been developed to a high degree. Such master artists as Michelangelo, Giotto, and da Vinci painted here, and many of their works still hang in Florence. Tuscan literary giants include Dante and Boccaccio. The poet Petrarch and astronomer Galileo added their genius.

Tuscany is one of Italy's largest regions, embracing ten provinces and the Isle of Elba, so it contains a varied landscape; mountainous in the Apennines but flat in the Arno Valley. The hilly land is suited to growing olive trees; vegetable gardens, fruit orchards, and cattle farms do better in the valley.

On an American menu, "florentine" usually means that spinach is used in a recipe. This doesn't necessarily follow in Florence itself, where the appellation simply means "in the style of Florence." Such a dish is apt to be straightforward, without a lot of fussing over. Excellent food is simply served, in a way that brings out its best natural qualities. A steak, for example, is often served pan-broiled with only a lemon wedge for garnish. On the Italian menu it is called "bistecca," which bears phonetic resemblance to the English term.

After a visit to the Uffizi Gallery in Florence, the visitor will be inspired to try some of the famous Florentine cuisine. He may encounter Fritto Misto, a mixture of variety meats, bits of vegetables, and veal cutlets. Fritto means "fried," and is similar to the English word "fritter." In Florence, Fritto Misto is sometimes followed by sweet fritters made with fruit in season.

Possibly because Italy has less space for cattle farming than we have in this country, small animals are more frequently used in Italian cooking. Rabbit, for example, is put to good use in Italian recipes. Lepre dolce-forte is popular in Florence.

Tortino di Carciofi, an artichoke-egg concoction, is worth adding to the recipe file. A quickly prepared dish, it produces excellent eating after a minimum of preparation.

To do Tuscany justice, the culinary tour should not end with Florence. Lucca, Siena, Pisa (home of the Leaning Tower), and the Mediterranean coast all offer a variety of good eating.

The wine usually associated with Tuscany is Chianti, the noblest being the Chianti classico in the straight-sided bottle bearing a gold cockerel on a gold background. Better known is the Chianti in the round-bottomed, straw-covered bottle. It is robust, ready to drink when purchased, a perfect partner for the heartiest dishes.

Artichoke Pie (Tortino di Carciofi alla Fiorentina)

1 package (9 ounces) frozen
   artichoke hearts
   Lemon juice
2 tablespoons olive oil
1½ tablespoons butter
   Flour
4 eggs
½ teaspoon salt
   Pinch pepper
2 tablespoons milk or water

1. Thinly slice the artichoke hearts vertically and spread out on paper towels. Pat dry when thawed, and drizzle with lemon juice.
2. Heat olive oil and butter in a 10-inch skillet with an ovenproof handle. Coat artichoke heart slices with flour and brown on both sides in hot fat.
3. Beat eggs slightly. Mix in salt, pepper, and milk. Pour over artichoke slices in skillet.
4. Bake at 350°F 5 to 10 minutes, or until egg mixture is set.

4 servings

Baked Fettuccine with Perch Florentine
(Fettuccine con Persici alla Fiorentina)

White Sauce
12 **small perch fillets**
1 **teaspoon salt**
¼ **teaspoon pepper**
2 **cups white wine**
3 **pounds spinach**
1 **pound fettuccine noodles, cooked according to package directions and drained**
¼ **cup grated Parmesan cheese**

1. Prepare sauce, place a piece of waxed paper directly on surface, and keep warm.
2. Wash and dry the fillets; place in a saucepan. Sprinkle with salt and pepper and pour in the wine. Simmer 15 minutes, or less, being sure fish remains intact.
3. Wash spinach. Place in a saucepan only with water that clings to leaves from washing. Cover saucepan and cook rapidly about 5 minutes, or until tender. Drain well and chop.
4. Arrange half the spinach in a 3-quart baking dish. Place half the fettuccine over spinach, and top with 6 fillets. Repeat layering with remaining spinach, fettuccine, and fish. Pour the warm sauce over all and sprinkle cheese on top.
5. Bake at 400°F 20 minutes, or until top is browned. Serve 2 fillets per person on a mound of fettuccine and spinach.

6 servings

White Sauce: Melt **5 tablespoons butter** in a saucepan. Blend in **5 tablespoons flour, 1 teaspoon salt,** and **⅛ teaspoon pepper;** heat until bubbly. Gradually add **2½ cups milk,** stirring until smooth. Bring to boiling and cook, stirring constantly, 1 to 2 minutes. Stir in **pinch nutmeg.**

About 2½ cups sauce

Broccoli Florentine (Broccoli alla Fiorentina)

1 **pound broccoli, washed and trimmed**
2 **tablespoons olive oil**
2 **cloves garlic, sliced thin**
¼ **teaspoon salt**
¼ **teaspoon pepper**

1. Split the heavy broccoli stalks (over ½ inch thick) lengthwise through stalks up to flowerets. Put into a small amount of boiling salted water. Cook, uncovered, 5 minutes, then cover and cook 10 to 15 minutes, or until broccoli is just tender.
2. Meanwhile, heat oil and garlic in a large skillet until garlic is lightly browned.
3. Drain broccoli and add to skillet; turn to coat with oil. Cook about 10 minutes, stirring occasionally. Season with salt and pepper. Serve hot.

4 servings

Broccoli Roman Style: Follow recipe for Broccoli Florentine. Omit cooking broccoli in boiling water. Cook broccoli in oil only 5 minutes. Add **1½ cups dry red wine** to skillet. Cook, covered, over low heat about 20 minutes, or until broccoli is tender; stir occasionally.

Spinach Sautéed in Oil: Follow recipe for Broccoli Florentine; substitute **2 cups chopped cooked spinach** for broccoli. Add spinach, **1 tablespoon chopped pinenuts or almonds,** and **1 tablespoon raisins** to oil mixture.

Mixed Fry *(Fritto Misto)*

½ pound calf's brains
2 cups water
1½ teaspoons vinegar or lemon juice
½ teaspoon salt
¼ cup flour
½ teaspoon salt
Pinch pepper
½ pound liver (beef, lamb, veal, or calf), sliced ¼ to ½ inch thick
2 cups all-purpose flour
1 teaspoon salt
¼ teaspoon pepper
1½ cups milk
3 eggs, well beaten
2 tablespoons melted shortening
Oil for frying
6 artichoke hearts (canned in water), drained
2 zucchini, washed and cut crosswise in 1-inch slices
3 stalks celery, cut in 3-inch pieces

1. Wash brains in cold water. Combine with 2 cups water, vinegar, and ½ teaspoon salt in a saucepan. Bring to boiling, reduce heat, and simmer gently 20 minutes.
2. Drain the brains and drop into cold water. Drain again and remove membranes. Separate into small pieces and set aside.
3. Combine ¼ cup flour, ½ teaspoon salt, and pinch pepper. Coat the liver with the flour mixture, cut into serving-size pieces, and set aside.
4. Combine 2 cups flour with 1 teaspoon salt and ¼ teaspoon pepper; set aside. Combine milk, eggs, and shortening. Gradually add the flour mixture to the liquid, beating until smooth.
5. Fill a deep saucepan one-half to two-thirds full with oil. Heat slowly to 360°F. Dip pieces of meat and the vegetables in the batter and fry in hot oil, being careful not to crowd the pieces. Fry about 5 minutes, or until golden brown, turning occasionally.
6. Hold cooked pieces over the hot oil to drain before placing on paper towels. Place on a warm platter and serve immediately.

6 servings

Manicotti Tuscan Style *(Manicotti alla Toscana)*

Egg Pasta Dough for Manicotti (page 32)
Tomato Sauce (page 32)
3 tablespoons butter
1 tablespoon olive oil
1 clove garlic, minced
6 mushrooms, minced
1 pound ground beef round
1 teaspoon salt
¼ teaspoon pepper
½ pound ricotta
¼ pound Parmesan cheese, grated

1. Prepare pasta dough and Tomato Sauce.
2. Heat butter and oil in a skillet. Add garlic; sauté until soft. Stir in mushrooms, beef, salt, and pepper. Cook until meat is brown, stirring often. Add ricotta and half the Parmesan cheese, blending well.
3. When dough squares are dry, spread ½ tablespoon of the beef mixture on each square and roll up tightly. Press edges together to seal, moistening edges with water if necessary. Filling must be sealed in completely, or it will fall out during the cooking in boiling water.
4. Cook manicotti in gently boiling salted water until just tender. Remove with a slotted spoon and drain. Arrange a layer of manicotti (about 30) in a buttered 3-quart casserole. Cover with Tomato Sauce and sprinkle with half of remaining Parmesan cheese. Arrange remaining manicotti crosswise in another layer, cover with Tomato Sauce, and sprinkle with remaining Parmesan cheese.
5. Bake at 350°F 25 minutes, or until cheese browns and sauce bubbles.

About 60 manicotti

Egg Pasta Dough for Manicotti

4 cups all-purpose flour
4 eggs, beaten
1½ teaspoons salt
2 teaspoons olive oil
Warm water (about ½ cup)

1. Put flour onto a board, make a well in center, and add eggs, salt, and olive oil. Mix until a soft dough is formed, adding warm water as needed.
2. Knead about 10 minutes until dough is smooth and elastic. Add more flour if dough is too soft.
3. Divide dough in quarters. Roll each quarter into as thin a sheet as possible. Cut the sheets into 3-inch squares. Dry on cloth or cloth-covered board for 1 hour before using.

About 1¾ pounds dough

Tomato Sauce

1 clove garlic
2 tablespoons olive oil
3 pounds fully ripe plum tomatoes, peeled, seeded, and diced; or use 9 cups canned peeled plum tomatoes, sieved
1 teaspoon salt
¼ teaspoon freshly ground black pepper
1 tablespoon dried basil

1. Peel garlic and cut in thirds. Put into a deep skillet with olive oil. Heat until garlic is browned. Flatten garlic and move it around in the oil. Discard garlic.
2. Add tomatoes all at one time to skillet. Mix in salt, pepper, and basil. Cook over low heat, stirring occasionally, about 10 minutes. Continue cooking, stirring occasionally, until sauce thickens (about 20 minutes).

About 6 cups sauce

Florentine Spinach (Spinaci alla Fiorentina)

2 pounds spinach
2 cups Medium White Sauce (page 83)
3 eggs, slightly beaten
3 tablespoons minced onion
½ teaspoon salt
½ teaspoon pepper

1. Wash spinach. Put into a large saucepan with only the water clinging to the leaves; cover. Cook rapidly about 5 minutes, or until tender. Drain well.
2. Prepare white sauce. Pour hot sauce into beaten eggs, stirring vigorously to blend. Set aside to cool to lukewarm.
3. Finely chop spinach. Combine spinach, sauce mixture, onion, salt, and pepper. Turn into a thoroughly greased 9-inch ring mold.
4. Set filled mold in a pan and pour hot water into pan to a depth of 1 inch.
5. Bake at 350°F 45 to 55 minutes, or until set.
6. Remove from oven; remove mold from water and let stand 5 minutes. Loosen spinach from mold and unmold onto a warm serving plate.

6 servings

Fruit Bread, Milan Style, 19, from Lombardy

THE MARCHES

The Marches can best be described as mountain country. And like mountains everywhere, they provide plenty of scenic interest, but little for the table. One exception is the marvel that appears spontaneously, with no human cultivation—the white truffle. Anyone lucky enough to have experienced a true "gourmet" Italian dinner has probably tasted it.

The beach resorts along the Adriatic coast are a tourist attraction, and so is the fish stew made from the varied catch from that shore. The basic combination includes squid and garlic, parsley and onion, embellished with other ingredients as available. Accompanied by a crusty loaf of bread, a salad, and a glass of wine, it is a complete meal.

A popular menu item in the region is porchetta, a whole suckling pig seasoned with sage and fennel, and stuffed with its own liver. The seasoned juices of the roasting pork flavor the liver and produce a dish with a flavor like liver paté.

The mountains of the Marches have made it difficult to earn a livelihood here, so modern ways have been relatively slow to take hold. Thus it's not unusual to encounter a recipe described as "peasant style." There is a veal recipe from the area that proves the point: Vitello alla Paesana.

Despite the obstacles to agriculture, wine production has thrived. Viticulture is indeed an uphill battle in the Marches, but once won, the product is a triumph. One white wine in particular, Verdicchio di Jesi, has won loyal friends both in and out of Italy. It comes in tall green bottles, and has a clean taste that goes well with the fish provided by the Adriatic.

Pork Roast Stuffed with Liver (Porchetta)

1 teaspoon fennel seed
2 cloves garlic, peeled
1 teaspoon salt
½ teaspoon sugar
½ teaspoon coarsely ground pepper
¾ teaspoon rubbed sage
   Boneless pork loin or loin end
      roast (about 3 pounds)
½ pound pork, lamb, or beef liver,
      cut in slices ⅓ inch thick
1 tablespoon cornstarch
1 cup cool beef broth

1. Using a mortar and pestle, crush the fennel seed. Add the garlic, salt, sugar, pepper, and sage. Crush until mixture becomes a rough paste.

2. Open pork roast and lay flat side down; cut the meat if necessary to make it lie flat. Rub surface of the roast with about half the garlic paste. Lay liver strips lengthwise over meat.

3. Roll the roast tightly lengthwise with seasoned surface inside. Tie with heavy string at 2-inch intervals. Rub remaining garlic paste on outside of roast. Place roast on a rack in a shallow baking pan.

4. Cook, uncovered, at 375°F until meat thermometer inserted in thickest part of the roast registers 170°F (about 1½ hours). Transfer roast to a serving platter and keep warm.

5. Remove rack from roasting pan and place pan over direct heat. Stir together the cornstarch and broth until blended. Stir into drippings in roasting pan. Cook over medium heat, stirring constantly, until sauce boils and thickens. Pour sauce into a serving bowl.

6. To serve, cut and remove strings from roast, and cut meat into thin slices.

About 8 servings

Ancona Fish Stew *(Brodetto Anconetana)*

2 pounds assorted fish (mullet, sole, and halibut fillets)
1 large onion, thinly sliced
½ cup olive oil
2 teaspoons salt
½ teaspoon pepper
   Pinch saffron
   Water (about 2 cups)
   Dry white wine (about 2 cups)

1. Cut fish fillets in 2½-inch pieces; set aside.
2. Sauté onion in olive oil until golden. Sprinkle in salt, pepper, and saffron. Add the fish and enough water and wine to cover the fish. Bring to boiling and cook over high heat 10 to 15 minutes.
3. Serve very hot in warmed soup bowls with crusts of fried bread, if desired.

6 servings

Veal Peasant Style *(Vitello alla Paesano)*

2 tablespoons butter
1 tablespoon olive oil
1 cup finely chopped onion
⅓ cup finely chopped celery
1½ to 2 pounds veal, cubed
1 teaspoon salt
¼ teaspoon pepper
4 tomatoes, peeled and coarsely chopped
   Several basil leaves or ¼ teaspoon dried basil leaves
¾ cup beef broth
2 tablespoons butter
1 pound fresh green peas, shelled, or 1 package (10 ounces) frozen green peas
3 carrots, diced
½ teaspoon salt
¾ cup hot water
1 tablespoon minced parsley

1. Heat 2 tablespoons butter and the olive oil in a Dutch oven or large saucepot. Add onion and celery; sauté 3 or 4 minutes.
2. Add meat and brown on all sides. Season with 1 teaspoon salt and the pepper. Stir in tomatoes and basil. Cover Dutch oven.
3. Cook at 275°F about 1¼ hours, or until meat is almost tender. Add broth, a little at a time, during cooking.
4. Heat 2 tablespoons butter in a saucepan. Stir in peas, carrots, ½ teaspoon salt, and water. Cook, covered, until vegetables are tender (about 15 minutes).
5. Skim off fat from meat. Stir in the cooked vegetables and parsley. Continue cooking in oven until meat is tender.
6. Serve meat surrounded with the vegetables and **small sautéed potatoes** on a heated platter. Pour sauce over all.

6 to 8 servings

 UMBRIA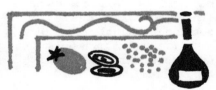

The Italian boot is a long projection of land into the sea; surrounded by water on three sides, only one region has no coastline—Umbria. But it boasts an inland shore around Lake Trasmieno, a gathering place for tourists and fishermen. Their daily catch, plus the bounty of other viands and wines, make it well worth a stop on the way from Venice to Rome.

Perugia is the capital of Umbria, and its major city, but it is less renowned outside the region than two smaller towns, Assisi and Orvieto.

Assisi is, of course, the birthplace of St. Francis, and the home of the order he founded in the thirteenth century. Pilgrims have followed the path to Assisi ever since.

Wine lovers recognize the name Orvieto in connection with one of Italy's finest wines. This village produces both white and rosé wines, and wines that are both dry and sweet.

Umbria has a long history. The Etruscans called it home long before the Romans established their empire, and they left behind many reminders of their occupation. Students of ancient civilization can have a field day in the area of Perugia.

The olive trees that decorate the Umbrian landscape provide the oil for many local dishes. A festive occasion in the region may produce a roast suckling pig or a dish of wild birds, adorned with the black truffles for which Umbria is famous.

Livestock is raised successfully in this inland region. Excellent cattle are bred in Umbria; thus a number of local dishes feature veal and beef. Pork is popular, too; la porchetta, or suckling pig, is a favorite roast meat.

Hunters in the spring and fall often bag wild pigeons. It is such a productive pastime that a special recipe, called Palombacci alla Perugina has been dedicated to it.

Pasta is, naturally, a fixture in the Umbrian menu as it is elsewhere in Italy. Spaghetti alla spoletina (spaghetti with truffle sauce) is credited to the town of Spoleto, but its popularity has spread beyond the borders of the region—and beyond Italy as well. Rice in various forms of risotto frequently gives the Umbrian meal its rib-sticking qualities.

Wild Pigeons Perugian (Palombacci alla Perugina)

3 pigeons or Rock Cornish hens
4 to 6 tablespoons olive oil
1 cup dry red wine
10 green olives
4 fresh sage leaves or ¼ teaspoon ground sage
½ teaspoon juniper berries
½ teaspoon salt
Dash pepper

1. Brown pigeons in 2 tablespoons hot olive oil in a Dutch oven, adding more oil if necessary. Stir in wine, 2 tablespoons olive oil, olives, sage, juniper berries, salt, and pepper.
2. Cook in a 300°F oven 50 to 60 minutes, or until pigeons are tender.

4 servings

Perugia Ham and Cheese Pie (Pizzetta alla Perugina)

2 cups all-purpose flour
½ teaspoon salt
¼ cup butter or margarine
2 eggs
3 tablespoons milk
1½ cups minced cooked ham
½ cup shredded Swiss cheese
½ cup diced Bel Paese cheese
1 egg yolk, slightly beaten

1. Combine flour and salt in a bowl. Cut in butter with pastry blender or two knives until pieces are small. Add eggs and stir in milk to form a soft dough. Knead dough lightly; divide in two equal portions.
2. Roll out one portion on a lightly floured surface into a rectangle large enough to line the bottom and sides of an 11×7-inch baking pan. Place dough in pan and cover with ham and cheese.
3. Bring dough on sides of pan down over the meat and cheese. Roll out the remaining dough to form an 11×7-inch rectangle and place on top of filling. Press edges of top crust with a fork to seal to bottom crust. Prick top with fork in several places, and brush with egg yolk.
4. Bake at 425°F 10 minutes. Turn oven control to 350°F and bake 10 minutes. Cut into rectangles and serve warm.

6 to 8 servings

LATIUM

The region of Latium richly deserves a visit, but all too often it is overlooked as the visitor hurries to the Eternal City located at its heart.

In Rome, we find a cuisine that has matured in keeping with its centuries of civilization. It is many-faceted, ranging from simple meals in the neighborhood trattoria to the gourmet fare offered in sophisticated dining rooms. Somewhere in-between are the sidewalk cafés where people-watching shares interest with the food.

One is apt to find a cross section of Italian cooking in Rome. Neapolitan pizza is available, but so is Venetian polenta. However, some dishes do have a distinctively Roman character. One of these is Fettuccine Alfredo, named for the Roman restaurateur whose establishment was on the itinerary of every food-minded traveler in the middle of this century. Alfredo would cut a colorful figure as he personally served the buttery noodles bathed in grated cheese to his guests, using serving pieces of gold.

Carciofi (artichokes) are often seen with the title "alla romano" on the menu. They are cooked in wine and olive oil with a trace of garlic, and may be served hot, cold, or in-between.

Abbachio, roasted milk-fed lamb, is popular in Rome. So are gnocchi, made either from cooked semolina or a flour and mashed-potato mixture. Meat sauce and a liberal cheese topping accompany the latter. Saltimbocca ("jump in the mouth," literally translated) is a Roman favorite, combining thin slices of veal with sage, ham, and a topping of mozzarella cheese.

Mozzarella stars in many Roman dishes, and another well-known cheese from the area is ricotta alla romana, which is made from whey and looks a little like cottage cheese. More an ingredient than a candidate for the cheese tray, ricotta is used in such dishes as lasagne.

Just as all roads lead to Rome, they also lead out, and the visitor is well rewarded who follows one, such as the Appian Way, for a look at the surrounding countryside.

The wines he will find may not be as monumental as those of some other regions, but an interesting story is told about one that comes from the slopes of Montefiascone. Years ago, a German cardinal is said to have sent an emissary ahead as he traveled to seek out inns with a good wine selection. The scout was to write "est" (Meaning "it is", implying "good") and "est est" if it was special. The wine of Montefiascone so impressed him that he left the graffiti "Est! Est!! Est!!!" on the door of the inn. The story has lived on, and so has the wine, with the name Est Est Est still applied.

While not offering any serious competition to Rome for the tourist's time, Tivoli is probably the second-most interesting city in Latium. It is often a side-trip for Roman visitors with an extra day. It outranks Rome in age by at least four centuries, and during the peak of the Roman Empire was a favorite resort getaway for the nobility.

The menus in the area will probably offer such temptations as cannelloni with meat filling, numerous veal and chicken dishes, and the ubiquitous noodle combinations. These will be recognizable by the "fettuccine" in the title.

Artichokes in Lemon (Carciofi con Limone)

1 can (14 ounces) artichoke hearts
3 tablespoons lemon juice
2 tablespoons olive oil
1 clove garlic, peeled and finely
    chopped
¼ teaspoon salt
⅛ teaspoon pepper

1. Drain artichoke hearts and place in refrigerator to chill. Combine remaining ingredients and chill.
2. When ready to serve, stir lemon-olive oil mixture and pour over artichoke hearts.

6 appetizer servings

Roman Egg Soup with Noodles
(Stracciatella con Pasta)

    4 cups chicken broth
 1½ tablespoons semolina or flour
 1½ tablespoons grated Parmesan
        cheese
    ⅛ teaspoon salt
    ⅛ teaspoon pepper
    4 eggs, well beaten
    1 cup cooked noodles
        Snipped parsley

1. Bring chicken broth to boiling.
2. Meanwhile, mix semolina, cheese, salt, and pepper together. Add to beaten eggs and beat until combined.
3. Add noodles to boiling broth, then gradually add egg mixture, stirring constantly. Continue stirring and simmer 5 minutes.
4. Serve topped with parsley.

4 servings

Roman Egg Soup with Spinach: Follow recipe for Roman Egg Soup with Noodles; omit noodles. Add ½ **pound chopped cooked fresh spinach** to broth before adding egg mixture.

Fettuccine Alfredo

    1 pound green noodles
        Boiling salted water
    2 tablespoons olive oil
    1 teaspoon chopped fresh basil
    1 clove garlic, minced
        Grated Parmesan cheese
        Butter

1. Cook noodles in boiling salted water until just tender; drain.
2. In a chafing dish, heat olive oil, basil, and garlic. Toss the noodles in hot oil with a fork until they are very hot.
3. Sprinkle generously with Parmesan cheese, adding a generous piece of butter, and toss again a moment before serving.

About 8 servings

Fettuccine al Burro Alfredo: Cook egg noodles in boiling salted water until barely tender, *al dente;* drain thoroughly. Bring quickly to the table in a heated serving bowl and rapidly toss and twirl with a generous amount of unsalted butter and finely grated Parmesan or Romano cheese so that the butter and cheese melt so quickly that the fettuccine can be served piping hot.

Lasagne I

        Tomato Sauce with Meat (page
            82)
    3 tablespoons olive oil
    1 pound ground beef
    1 pound lasagne noodles, cooked
            and drained
    ¾ pound mozzarella cheese, thinly
            sliced
    2 hard-cooked eggs, sliced
    ¼ cup grated Parmesan cheese
    ½ teaspoon pepper
    1 cup ricotta

1. Prepare sauce, allowing 4½ hours for cooking.
2. Heat olive oil in a skillet. Add ground beef and cook until browned, separating into small pieces.
3. Spread ½ cup sauce in a 2-quart baking dish. Top with a layer of noodles and half the mozzarella cheese. Spread half the ground beef and half the egg slices on top. Sprinkle on half the Parmesan cheese and ¼ teaspoon pepper. Top with ½ cup ricotta.
4. Beginning with sauce, repeat layering, ending with ricotta. Top ricotta with ½ cup sauce. Arrange over this the remaining lasagne noodles. Top with more sauce.
5. Bake at 350°F about 30 minutes, or until mixture is bubbling. Let stand 5 to 10 minutes to set the layers. Cut in squares and serve topped with remaining sauce.

6 to 8 servings

Gnocchi

Tomato Meat Sauce (page 84)
3 medium (about 1 pound)
    potatoes, pared and quartered
1¾ cups sifted all-purpose flour
Grated Parmesan cheese

1. Prepare sauce, allowing 4½ hours for cooking.
2. While sauce is cooking, place the potatoes in enough boiling salted water to cover. Cook, covered, about 20 minutes, or until tender when pierced with a fork. Drain. Dry potatoes by shaking in pan over low heat.
3. Mash or rice the potatoes with a potato masher, food mill, or ricer that has been scalded with boiling water. Keep the potatoes hot.
4. Place the flour in a bowl, make a well in the center, and add the mashed potatoes. Mix well to make a soft dough. Turn dough onto lightly floured surface and knead 5 to 8 minutes until it is smooth and elastic.
5. Break off small pieces of dough and, using palms of hands, roll to pencil thickness. Cut into ¾-inch pieces. Curl each piece by pressing lightly with the index finger and pulling the finger along the dough toward you. Gnocchi may also be shaped by pressing each piece with a lightly floured fork.
6. Gradually add the gnocchi to 3 quarts boiling water, cooking about half at a time. Boil rapidly, uncovered, 8 to 10 minutes, or until gnocchi are tender and float to the surface.
7. Drain gnocchi in a colander or large sieve, and mix with 2 cups Tomato Meat Sauce, top with remaining sauce, and sprinkle generously with cheese. Serve immediately.

About 6 servings

Meat-Stuffed Manicotti

2 tablespoons olive oil
½ pound fresh spinach, washed,
    dried, and finely chopped
2 tablespoons chopped onion
½ teaspoon salt
½ teaspoon oregano
½ pound ground beef
2 tablespoons fine dry bread
    crumbs
1 egg, slightly beaten
1 can (6 ounces) tomato paste
8 manicotti shells (two thirds of a
    5½-ounce package), cooked
    and drained
1½ tablespoons butter, softened
    (optional)
1 to 2 tablespoons grated
    Parmesan or Romano cheese
    (optional)
Mozzarella cheese, shredded

1. Heat olive oil in a skillet. Add spinach, onion, salt, oregano, and meat. Mix well, separating meat into small pieces. Cook, stirring frequently, until meat is no longer pink.
2. Set aside to cool slightly. Add bread crumbs, egg, and 2 tablespoons tomato paste; mix well. Stuff manicotti with mixture. Put side by side in a greased 2-quart baking dish. If desired, spread butter over stuffed manicotti and sprinkle with the grated cheese.
3. Spoon remaining tomato paste on top of the manicotti down the center of the dish. Sprinkle mozzarella cheese on top of tomato paste. Cover baking dish.
4. Bake at 425°F 12 to 15 minutes, or until mozzarella melts.

4 servings

Saltimbocca *(Sliced Ham and Veal with Wine)*

4 large, thinly sliced veal cutlets
Salt and pepper
4 large, very thin slices ham or
   prosciutto
Dried sage leaves
Olive oil
¼ cup (2 ounces) Marsala

1. Place veal slices on a cutting board and pound with a mallet until very thin. Divide each slice into 2 or 3 pieces.
2. Season veal with salt and pepper.
3. Cut ham into pieces the same size as veal.
4. Place a sage leaf on each piece of veal and top with a slice of ham. Secure with a wooden pick.
5. Heat several tablespoons olive oil in a skillet; add the meat and cook slowly until golden brown on both sides. Remove meat to heated platter and keep warm.
6. Scrape residue from bottom of pan; add the Marsala and simmer over low heat several minutes. Pour over meat and serve.

4 servings

ABRUZZI E MOLISE

On the east coast of Italy, directly east of Rome, lies the region made up of two provinces, Abruzzi and Molise. Civilization focused on Rome, and left these two to remain as country cousins.

Thus, the cuisine of Abruzzi e Molise is less refined than that of Latium, and the austere terrain is not conducive to farming. However, the Apennine Mountains that run through the region have offering for skiers and scenery lovers.

In addition to the mountainous nature of the land, a harsh climate and occasional earthquakes have combined to frustrate farming. The raising of sheep is more successful, and they provide both meat and wool.

During the height of the Roman Empire, the coastal town of Pescara was a center for trade with the Orient. Thoroughly modernized today, it retains little of that ancient grandeur, but it is an interesting stopover. A visitor to Pescara will probably be offered a sampling of the fish (pesce) from which the name of the city is derived.

Maccheroni alla Chitarra ("guitar") is said to have originated in this region. Maccheroni, or the pasta for this dish, is made by laying the thin dough over a wooden frame strung with steel wires, making it look something like a guitar. A rolling pin is passed over the dough, producing thin strips. The Abruzzian cook boils it to tenderness and serves it with a tomato sauce to which meat, cheese, or other additions are made, depending on what is available.

All of the coastal towns have their fish soups, and those of Abruzzi e Molise have an individuality all their own. Most combine several kinds of fish with onions, tomatoes, and seasonings, including bay leaves and parsley. The distinctive local addition is the white vinegar for which Abruzzi is famous.

Tiny Turnovers *(Cuscinetti di Teramo)*

2 cups all-purpose flour
2 teaspoons sugar
½ teaspoon salt
3 tablespoons cooking oil
½ to ¾ cup white wine
¾ cup marmalade or jam
   Slivered almonds
   Oil for frying heated to 370°F

1. Combine flour, sugar, salt, oil, and wine, mixing just enough to make a tender dough. Knead briefly and roll very thin (⅛ inch or less). Cut into 3¼-inch rounds.
2. Place 1 teaspoon marmalade mixed with a few slivered almonds on each round. Moisten edges of rounds, fold in half, and press together to seal. Spread on a tray or cutting board and let stand several hours to dry a little.
3. Fry in hot oil until golden. Remove, using slotted spoon, and drain on paper towels. Serve warm.

36 turnovers

Egg Noodles Abruzzi (Maccheroni alla Chitarra)

1 tablespoon butter
¼ cup olive oil
1 pound ground lamb
2 green peppers, chopped
1 teaspoon salt
¼ teaspoon pepper
½ cup dry white wine
2 large tomatoes, peeled and
    coarsely chopped
1 pound egg noodles

1. Heat butter and oil in a large skillet. Stir in lamb and green peppers; season with salt and pepper. Brown the meat slightly, stirring occasionally.
2. Add wine and simmer until liquid is almost evaporated. Stir in tomatoes and simmer mixture 30 minutes, or until sauce is thick.
3. Cook noodles according to package directions; drain. Place noodles on a hot platter, pour sauce over noodles, and serve.

4 to 6 servings

Stuffed Pancakes (Scrippelle Imbusse)

4 eggs
1 cup all-purpose flour
½ teaspoon salt
¾ cup water
    Cooking oil
½ cup freshly grated Parmesan or
    Romano cheese
1 cup minced prosciutto
1 cup chicken broth

1. Beat eggs well in a medium-size mixing bowl. Gradually add flour and salt; mix well. When the mixture is smooth and creamy, add water, more if needed to make a thin batter.
2. Heat a 5-inch skillet and brush with oil. Pour in 2 tablespoons batter, spreading over bottom of skillet to form a thin pancake. As soon as bubbles appear on the top, turn and brown other side.
3. Continue making pancakes, greasing the skillet between each one. Combine cheese with prosciutto; sprinkle each pancake with about 1½ tablespoons of the mixture. Roll up pancakes tightly and place side by side in a shallow baking dish.
4. Bring chicken broth to boiling and pour over rolled pancakes. Cover the dish and set in a hot place (a heated oven with the heat turned off) for a few minutes, so the broth will be partially absorbed. Serve immediately.

16 filled pancakes

 CAMPANIA

The capital of Italy, at least in the food sense, may very well be Naples. Situated in the heart of rich farming country and well provided with local wines, cheeses, and sausages, Naples has evolved a style of cooking well worth a trip to the coast of Campania. Embellished with olive oil and tomatoes, the cooking of southern Italy is more colorful and often more highly seasoned than the creamy cooking of the north.

Inland in Campania, golden sunshine and fertile soil combine to produce some of Italy's finest fruits and vegetables. The tomato grown so lavishly in this region was actually introduced from the New World, but has been incorporated into so many Italian dishes that it earned its naturalization long ago.

Dairy farming prospers in Campania, but with some local differences. Water buffalo provide the milk for the mozzarella that finds its way into so many Neapolitan dishes.

Mention "Italian cooking" in America, and what usually comes to mind is Neapolitan cooking, rich with tomato sauces, generously spiced, and based on pasta. Pizza was born in Naples. Evidently more cooks emigrated from Naples than from the other Italian regions, because, as we have seen, many other regional styles do exist. But thanks to the Neapolitan chefs who played ambassador, and also to the ease with which their dishes are reproduced, they dominate the Italian-American cuisine.

Spaghetti is one of the most popular pasta forms in Campania. Combining it with the plentiful clams of the region produces a dish called spaghetti alla vongole. Lasagne shares pasta honors, and in Campania is often served imbottita (stuffed).

Melanzane (eggplant) is given lavish attention in this region. Sometimes it is treated like lasagne, layered with a meat sauce and mozzarella, topped with Parmesan. At other times it is sautéed and sprinkled with Parmesan.

But excellent as Neapolitan cooking is, there are other attractions in Campania. The islands of Capri and Ischia that stand guard to the entrance of Naples are among the most beautiful in the Mediterranean. Located as they are, such seafood specialties as zuppa di pesce are sure to be featured on their menus.

Visitors to Campania often visit Pompeii, that first-century town destroyed by the erupting Vesuvius. And if they continue inland along the Amalfi Drive, they are rewarded with some of the finest scenery in all of Europe. When they reach the port of Amalfi itself, they receive another bonus from the rich Neapolitan menu.

The output of wines in Campania is great and the style is robust, well suited to the food of the region. Rosso wine is made to order for the "red" food. In contrast, one white wine stands out— lacrima Christi (tears of Christ) from the southern slopes of Mt. Vesuvius.

Pasta with Beans Sorrento Style
(Conchigliette con Fagioli alla Sorrento)

2 cups dried Great Northern beans
5 cups water
1 teaspoon salt
1 cup chopped celery
1 cup chopped onion
3 tablespoons olive oil
1 teaspoon salt
6 ripe tomatoes, peeled and diced
1 tablespoon chopped Italian
   parsley
4 fresh basil leaves, chopped, or 1
   teaspoon dried basil
½ pound conchigliette

1. Rinse beans and put into a heavy saucepot or kettle. Add water and bring rapidly to boiling; boil 2 minutes and remove from heat. Cover; set aside 1 hour.
2. Stir 1 teaspoon salt into beans, cover, and bring to boiling. Cook until beans are nearly done, but still firm (about 2 hours). Drain and set aside.
3. Sauté the celery and onion in olive oil until soft. Sprinkle in 1 teaspoon salt, then stir in tomatoes, parsley, and basil.
4. Simmer 15 minutes, uncovered. Add the beans to tomato mixture; stir well. Cook the conchigliette according to package directions, drain, and stir into bean mixture. Serve in hot soup bowls.

4 to 6 servings

Chicken Vesuvio *(Pollo alla Vesuviana)*

1 broiler-fryer chicken (2 to 3
    pounds), cut in pieces
½ cup flour
1½ teaspoons salt
¼ teaspoon pepper
½ cup olive oil
2 tablespoons olive oil
1 clove garlic, sliced
2 tablespoons Marsala
½ teaspoon chopped parsley
    Deep-Fried Potatoes (page 78)

1. Coat chicken pieces with a mixture of flour, salt, and pepper.
2. Heat ½ cup oil in a large skillet. Add chicken pieces and brown on all sides. Put into a large, shallow baking dish.
3. Heat 2 tablespoons oil and garlic until garlic is lightly browned. Add Marsala and parsley; mix well. Pour over chicken in baking dish.
4. Bake at 325°F about 45 minutes, or until chicken is tender; turn once.
5. Prepare potatoes and place around edges of baking dish.

4 servings

Neapolitan Pork Chops
(Costatelle di Maiale alla Napoletana)

2 tablespoons olive oil
1 clove garlic, minced
6 pork rib or loin chops, cut about
    ¾ to 1 inch thick
1 teaspoon salt
¼ teaspoon pepper
1 pound mushrooms, cleaned and
    sliced
2 green peppers, cleaned and
    chopped
½ cup canned tomatoes, sieved
3 tablespoons dry white wine

1. Heat oil in a large, heavy skillet. Add garlic and cook until lightly browned.
2. Season chops with salt and pepper. Put chops in skillet and brown on both sides.
3. Add mushrooms, green pepper, sieved tomato, and wine. Cover and cook over low heat about 1 hour, or until tender.

6 servings

Stuffed Eggplant *(Melanzane Ripiene)*

3 medium eggplants (about 3
    pounds)
1½ teaspoons salt
1 cup boiling water
¼ cup butter
1 cup chopped onion
2 cups coarsely chopped peeled
    tomatoes
1 to 2 teaspoons salt
¼ teaspoon pepper
1 teaspoon dried basil
½ teaspoon oregano

1. Cut the eggplants in half lengthwise. Make several cuts into the pulp, being careful not to pierce skin. Sprinkle cut sides with 1½ teaspoons salt. Let stand 30 minutes.
2. Pat eggplant halves dry with paper towels. Place flat-side down in a baking pan. Add boiling water.
3. Bake at 375°F, uncovered, 15 minutes, or until just tender. Cool on wire rack. Scoop out pulp, leaving ¼-inch-thick shell walls. Chop pulp coarsely and drain. Set pulp and shells aside.
4. Melt ¼ cup butter in a large skillet. Add the onion and sauté about 5 minutes, or until golden. Stir in tomatoes, 1 to 2 teaspoons salt, pepper, basil, ½ teaspoon oregano, ham, ½

2 cups chopped cooked ham
1 cup fine dry bread crumbs
¼ teaspoon oregano
¼ cup butter, melted
6 slices mozzarella cheese, halved
12 anchovy fillets
2 tablespoons chopped parsley

cup of the bread crumbs, and the eggplant pulp. Simmer, covered, 5 minutes.

5. Fill eggplant shells with mixture, mounding slightly. Place in a shallow baking pan. Combine remaining ½ cup bread crumbs, ¼ teaspoon oregano, and melted butter; sprinkle over each eggplant.

6. Place 2 pieces cheese on top of each eggplant half. Lay 2 anchovy fillets on each half.

7. Bake at 375°F about 15 minutes, or until cheese melts and filling is heated through. Sprinkle each half with 1 teaspoon chopped parsley.

6 servings

White Clam Sauce *(Salsa alla Vongole)*

¼ cup olive oil
1 clove garlic, thinly sliced
¼ cup water
½ teaspoon chopped parsley
½ teaspoon salt
¼ teaspoon oregano
¼ teaspoon pepper
1 cup (8-ounce can) whole littleneck clams with juice

1. Heat oil and garlic in a skillet until garlic is lightly browned.

2. Remove from heat. Add water, parsley, and dry seasonings; mix well. Stir in clams with juice. Heat thoroughly.

3. Serve hot on **cooked spaghetti** or **macaroni**.

About 1½ cups sauce

Red Clam Sauce: Follow recipe for White Clam Sauce. Sieve **3½ cups canned tomatoes,** stir in with water and seasonings, and simmer about 10 minutes. Add clams and heat.

About 5 cups sauce

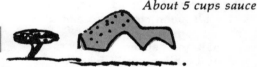

APULIA

Naples dominates the culinary horizon of southern Italy, but the region of Apulia probably ranks right behind it, thanks to its fortunate climate and acres of fertile land.

Apulia is the heel of the Italian boot, looking like a peninsula on a peninsula. Bordering on the sea for almost five hundred miles, it has generous access to seafood from both the Adriatic and Ionian waters. Swordfish, eels, mackerel, anchovies, and many more are in the Apulian haul, but it is for the oysters and mussels that the region is best known. Prolific oyster beds lie near the port town of Taranto; the Italians are said to have been the first to cultivate oyster farms.

It is the seafood that is credited with bringing the high population density to the coastal regions of Apulia. Inland, much of the land is used for wheat farming. Apulia is wheat country, the bread basket of Italy, and the people of Apulia

treat their daily bread reverently.

Even the baking of the bread has become a ritual. Dough from the baking in one household is saved for the starter for baking in the next; this community sharing of the leavener has great meaning for the people. Because of this passing of dough from one baker to the next, it is said that the yeast of Apulia has been alive for generations.

Not for their beef, but for their dairy products, are the cattle of Apulia prized. A dish that combines both the bread and cheese of Apulia is the locally popular mozzarella alla carrozza—translated, "mozzarella in a carriage."

The cooking style of Apulia is characterized by pastas served with meat sauces to which vegetables have been added. Combinations that might seem discordant to the American taste, such as cabbages or turnips in the meat and tomato sauce, are favored here.

Pasta with Potatoes (Lumachine con Patate)

2 white onions, chopped
2 tablespoons olive oil
2 tablespoons butter
1 pound potatoes, pared and diced
2 pounds very ripe tomatoes, peeled and coarsely chopped
1½ teaspoons salt
½ teaspoon freshly ground pepper
1 tablespoon minced Italian parsley
1 pound lumachine
6 tablespoons grated Romano cheese

1. Sauté onions in oil and butter until soft. Stir in potatoes and simmer, covered, 15 minutes.
2. Stir in tomatoes, salt, pepper, and parsley. Simmer, covered, 25 minutes, then uncovered 10 minutes, stirring often.
3. Cook lumachine according to package directions; drain. Add to tomatoes and potatoes; mix well. Blend in 4 tablespoons cheese.
4. Serve immediately in hot soup bowls with remaining cheese sprinkled on top.

6 to 8 servings

Eggplant Pugliese Style (Melanzane alla Pugliese)

3 medium-size eggplants (about ½ pound each)
2 tablespoons olive oil
1 tablespoon chopped parsley
1 medium onion, chopped
1 clove garlic, peeled and chopped
1½ cups chopped cooked meat (see Note)
½ cup fine dry bread crumbs
1 tablespoon chopped pinenuts or almonds
Salt and pepper
3 or 4 tablespoons olive oil
1 can (8 ounces) tomato sauce

1. Wash and dry eggplants; remove stems. Cut eggplants in half crosswise, and scoop out most of the pulp; reserve pulp.
2. Heat 2 tablespoons olive oil in a skillet. Sauté pulp, parsley, onion, and garlic. Add meat, bread crumbs, and pinenuts. Season with salt and pepper; set aside.
3. Heat 3 or 4 tablespoons olive oil in another skillet. Cook eggplant shells in hot oil until the skins start to brown. Fill each half with the meat mixture. Pour tomato sauce over each half and cover skillet.
4. Cook eggplant slowly 20 to 30 minutes, or until tender.
5. If desired, place eggplant in a serving dish, add more tomato sauce, and keep in warm oven until ready to serve.

4 to 6 servings

Note: If desired, ¾ pound uncooked chopped beef, lamb, or pork may be used. Sauté with pulp, parsley, onion, and garlic until browned before combining with other ingredients.

Vegetable Omelet (Frittata)

3 tablespoons olive oil
½ cup chopped onion
½ cup sliced mushrooms
½ cup sliced zucchini
10 frozen artichoke heart halves, thawed
1 teaspoon salt
¼ teaspoon freshly ground black pepper
6 eggs
¼ cup canned tomato sauce

1. Heat oil in a 9-inch skillet with an oven-proof handle. Sauté onion 5 minutes. Add mushrooms, zucchini, and artichoke heart halves; cook 10 minutes over low heat. Sprinkle ½ teaspoon salt and ⅛ teaspoon pepper over vegetables.
2. Beat eggs with remaining ½ teaspoon salt and ⅛ teaspoon pepper; pour over vegetables. Spoon tomato sauce over the top.
3. Bake at 350°F 15 minutes, or until eggs are set. Cut in wedges and serve immediately.

4 to 6 servings

BASILICATA

Basilicata, the "spats" on the Italian boot, has its problems when it comes to stocking the larder. Like much of southern Italy, it is desert country, inviting neither large human settlements nor farming. Like Calabria, it has been subjected to earthquakes, so there is little of the ancient architecture remaining to draw attention to the region, or to encourage newcomers.

But the natives who have endured are a hardy lot. They are the vital product of a melting pot that embraced Arabs, Greeks, Byzantines, and a mix of other Europeans and Asians. They are dark haired and hard working, as they must be to win a living from this reluctant soil. Water is scarce, and must often be carried a distance.

Because meat is not plentiful, the people of Basilicata have turned their ingenuity to pasta and vegetable dishes. As in all southern Italian cooking, the tomato is important.

Four centuries ago, the tomato was introduced into Italy from the New World. The Italians named it pomodoro, which means "golden apple," because those early tomatoes were yellow. The sun in the southern regions smiles on the small varieties featured in Basilicatan cooking.

As in Calabria, white Malvasia wine is produced in this region. So is the sparkling Spumante, Italy's answer to champagne.

Veal and Peppers Basilicata Style
(Vitello e Pepe alla Basilicata)

2 tablespoons butter
1 tablespoon lard
1½ pounds boneless veal leg, rump, or shoulder roast, cut in 1-inch pieces
1 teaspoon salt
⅛ teaspoon pepper
1 medium-size onion, sliced
4 large ripe tomatoes
1 tablespoon chopped basil leaves or 1 teaspoon dried sweet basil
4 large firm green or red peppers
3 tablespoons olive oil

1. Heat butter and lard in skillet over medium heat. Add meat and brown on all sides. Stir in salt, pepper, and onion; cook 5 minutes.
2. Cut tomatoes in half, squeeze out seeds, chop pulp, and add with basil to meat. Cover and simmer 20 minutes.
3. Cut out stems, remove seeds, and clean peppers. Cut in quarters, lengthwise. Fry peppers in hot olive oil about 10 minutes, or until softened. Add to meat, cover, and simmer 30 minutes, or until meat is tender. Serve hot.

4 servings

Artichokes Basilicata Style (Carciofi alla Basilicata)

1 package (9 ounces) frozen artichoke hearts
1 tablespoon lemon juice
½ cup fine dry bread crumbs
1 tablespoon grated Parmesan or Romano cheese
1 teaspoon chopped fresh basil leaves or ½ teaspoon dried basil
1 egg
½ teaspoon salt
⅛ teaspoon pepper
½ cup olive oil

1. Slice artichoke hearts vertically into thin slices. Spread out on paper towels to thaw. Sprinkle with lemon juice and let stand 30 minutes.
2. Combine bread crumbs, cheese, and basil. Beat egg with salt and pepper. Dip artichoke heart slices in egg, then roll in bread-crumb mixture.
3. Heat olive oil in skillet. Add artichoke heart slices and cook over low heat until browned. Serve while crisp.

3 or 4 servings

Green Beans Basilicata Style
(Fagiolini alla Basilicata)

1½ pounds fresh green beans
1 teaspoon salt
2 quarts boiling water
¼ cup chopped onion
2 tablespoons olive oil
½ teaspoon salt
⅛ teaspoon pepper
2 tablespoons chopped fresh mint
   or basil leaves
3 tablespoons wine vinegar

1. Wash beans and break off ends. Leave whole or cut as desired.
2. Add 1 teaspoon salt to boiling water, stir in beans, cover, and bring to boiling. Cook 10 minutes, or until crisp-tender.
3. While beans are cooking, sauté onion in olive oil until transparent (about 8 minutes). When beans are done cooking, drain and add to onion. Season with ½ teaspoon salt and the pepper. Add mint leaves and vinegar; toss gently. Serve while hot.

4 to 6 servings

CALABRIA

Calabria, the toe of the Italian boot, is mountainous. It has been called "Italy's Switzerland," which makes for beautiful scenery, but difficult farming. Add to that occasional earthquakes, and you can appreciate what a challenge the farmer faces in Calabria.

Despite these odds, he has managed to produce quantities of eggplants, and the chef has complied with a variety of recipes to make use of them. Even those Americans who claim to "hate eggplant" must admit that this says something for the Calabrian ingenuity, considering the relatively short supply of local foods. One of the Calabrian ways with eggplant is melanzane al funghetto, eggplant slices topped with a mixture of minced garlic and other seasonings, then baked.

While not friendly to most crops, the hillsides of Calabria are covered with ancient olive trees; thus cooking in olive oil is common. And carrying the comparison to Switzerland one step farther,

dairy farming is productive in this region.

Every Italian region has its pasta, and Calabria is no exception. Fusilli, the curly spaghetti, is served here in a sauce with rolls of beef round alongside.

Thanks to its long shoreline, Calabria is blessed with a bounty of seafood. Tuna and swordfish are local favorites. Calabrians enjoy the fish fresh from the sea; Americans can substitute canned tuna when sampling their dishes.

Meat is in rather short supply in this region, but a pair of pork specialties is associated with Calabria. These are capocollo, somewhat like our Canadian bacon, and soprassato, a thick, spicy sausage flecked with pistachio nuts.

Some good wines are produced in Calabria; as often happens, vineyards flourish there in soil that would discourage other roots. Malvasia, a well-known white wine, is produced here. So is ciro di Calabria, a popular red table wine.

Buttered Carrots *(Carote al Burro)*

1½ pounds carrots
1 teaspoon sugar
½ teaspoon salt
⅛ teaspoon pepper
3 tablespoons butter
¾ cup water
1 tablespoon chopped parsley

1. Pare carrots and cut into julienne strips. Place in a large, heavy saucepan with sugar, salt, pepper, butter, and water. Cover.
2. Bring to boiling, then simmer 10 to 15 minutes, or until carrots are tender and moisture is evaporated. Remove cover to evaporate moisture, if necessary.
3. Turn carrots into a serving bowl and sprinkle with parsley.

6 servings

Country Style Chicken *(Pollo alla Paesana)*

1 frying chicken (about 3
    pounds), cut in serving pieces
2 tablespoons butter
2 tablespoons olive oil
1 medium-size onion, sliced
1 teaspoon salt
⅛ teaspoon pepper
1 pound zucchini
2 large green peppers
1½ tablespoons olive oil
1 teaspoon chopped basil leaves,
    or ¼ teaspoon dried sweet
    basil
½ cup dry white wine

1. In a large skillet, brown the chicken in butter and 2 tablespoons olive oil. Place onion around chicken; sprinkle with salt and pepper. Cover and cook slowly about 15 minutes.
2. While chicken is cooking, wash and cut zucchini in ½-inch-thick slices. Wash peppers; remove stems and seeds. Rinse in cold water and slice lengthwise into 1-inch-wide strips.
3. In another skillet, heat 1½ tablespoons olive oil and sauté zucchini and peppers until soft (about 10 minutes). Sprinkle with basil. Transfer vegetables to skillet with chicken and pour in wine.
4. Simmer, covered, about 15 minutes, or until chicken is very tender and vegetables are cooked.

About 4 servings

With a civilization older than that on the Italian mainland, although less well known, Sicilians are proud of their land. Traces remain of Carthaginian architecture, Greek temples, Roman roads and bridges, Byzantine churches, and pointed Turkish mosques—a silent but eloquent reminder of the march of history across the island.

Sicilian cooking has been influenced by each of these cultures. Before the time of Christ, Greek cooking was introduced and had a profound impact. The cooking became so refined that to have a Sicilian cook was a status symbol on the mainland during the Roman Empire.

Sicily enjoys a paradisiacal climate from fall through spring, luring tourists to such centers as Palermo, the capital, Taormina, and Syracuse. It is also conducive to the growth of almost tropical vegetation. Sicilian vegetables in Italian markets are recognized as the first sign of spring. Citrus fruits, olives, and grapes do well in Sicilian soil. A considerable amount of wheat is grown on the island, too, providing flour for the bread and pasta that are mainstays of the diet.

One form of Sicilian bread is baked in a round loaf, a bequest of the Greek conquerors. This is made at home in an igloo-shaped oven familiar to Sicilian kitchens.

For everyday meals, pasta shares honors with bread. One popular Sicilian dish, called minestra di lenticchi, combines pasta with lentils. Many such dishes combining two or more vegetable foods, inadequate in protein by themselves, together provide a more complete body-building diet. This has been important in a land where meat is sometimes scarce.

Eggs have furnished their share of protein and good eating, too. In one Sicilian specialty, farsumagru, hard-cooked eggs go into a filling for a meat roll which stretches the number of servings. Arancine are meat-stuffed rice balls with a bread coating, maximizing the number of servings from a small amount of meat.

Since it is an island, seafood dishes have been developed to a high degree in Sicily. One local specialty is pasta alla sarde, a combination of cooked macaroni layered with tender stalks of fennel and small sardines. Anchovies, raisins, and skillful seasoning make it a memorable dish, served cold in wedges.

The gnarled olive trees that adorn the Sicilian landscape are more than picturesque; they have provided cooking oil for centuries. Virgin oil, that which rises to the top after the olives are pressed, is used for salads and in other dishes; the heavier oil which settles to the bottom is used as a shortening.

Perhaps it is in the dessert department that Sicily achieves its greatest success. Rich ricotta desserts, such as cassata alla siciliana and the cannoli are famous far beyond Sicily's shores. Ice creams, ices, and sherbets are also credited to the island. Cakes in beautiful shapes, often filled with fruit or chocolate and crowned with tempting glazes, are the hallmark of the Sicilian bakery.

Almond nougats and sugar marzipan also help to satisfy the Sicilian sweet tooth.

The wines of Sicily are famous and are said to date back to the cult of Dionysus in ancient Greece. Among the best known are the dessert wines, Marsala and Malvasia.

Spaghetti Sicilian Style (Spaghetti alla Siciliana)

½ cup olive oil
2 cloves garlic, peeled and quartered
½ medium-size eggplant, pared and diced
6 large ripe tomatoes, peeled and coarsely chopped
2 green peppers
1 tablespoon chopped fresh basil or ½ teaspoon dried sweet basil
1 tablespoon capers
4 anchovy fillets, cut in small pieces
12 ripe olives, pitted and halved
1 teaspoon salt
¼ teaspoon pepper
1 pound spaghetti

1. Heat olive oil in a skillet; stir in garlic. Remove garlic from oil when brown. Stir eggplant and tomatoes into skillet; simmer 30 minutes.
2. Cut peppers vertically in half; remove membrane and seeds. Place peppers under broiler, skin side up, to loosen skins. Peel off skin, slice peppers, and add to tomato mixture.
3. Stir basil, capers, anchovies, olives, salt, and pepper into tomato mixture. Cover the skillet and simmer 10 minutes, or until sauce is well blended and is thickened.
4. Cook spaghetti according to package directions and drain. Immediately pour sauce over spaghetti and serve.

About 6 servings

Baked Rice Balls (Arancine)

1½ pounds ground beef
1 small onion, chopped
1 can (6 ounces) tomato paste
¾ cup water
1 teaspoon salt
⅛ teaspoon pepper
1 tablespoon chopped parsley
6 cups cooked rice, hot
½ cup grated Romano cheese
¼ cup butter
1 cup all-purpose flour
2 eggs, slightly beaten
All-purpose flour (1 to 1½ cups)
3 eggs, slightly beaten
2 cups fine dry bread crumbs
1 can (8 ounces) tomato sauce

1. Brown ground beef with onion in a skillet. Add tomato paste, stir, and cook 5 minutes. Add water, salt, pepper, and parsley. Mix well and cool about 15 minutes.
2. Combine rice, cheese, butter, 1 cup flour, and 2 eggs. Mix until butter is melted and ingredients are well blended.
3. With well-floured hands, shape some rice into a small ball. Flatten slightly and top with 1 tablespoon of the meat mixture. Top with more rice to cover meat, and make into a ball the size of a small orange.
4. Hold the ball over a shallow pan filled with about 1 cup flour; add more flour when needed. Sprinkle rice ball with flour while gently packing and turning in palm of hand.
5. Carefully dip ball in beaten eggs, then roll gently in bread crumbs to coat. Repeat with remaining rice. Place finished rice balls in a jelly-roll pan or baking sheet lined with aluminum foil.
6. Bake at 350°F 30 minutes. While rice balls are baking, stir tomato sauce into meat sauce and heat. Serve sauce over baked rice balls.

7 or 8 servings

Stuffed Artichokes Sicilian
(Carciofi Imbottiti alla Siciliana)

4 medium artichokes
1 teaspoon salt
⅔ cup fine dry bread crumbs
1 clove garlic, peeled and thinly
   sliced
1 teaspoon grated Parmesan cheese
1 teaspoon chopped parsley
1 teaspoon salt
¾ teaspoon pepper
2 cloves garlic, peeled and thinly
   sliced
1 tablespoon chopped parsley
2 cups boiling water
2 tablespoons olive oil

1. Cut off 1 inch from the top and base of each artichoke. Remove lower outer leaves. If desired, snip off tips of remaining leaves. Cover with cold water and add 1 teaspoon salt. Let stand 5 to 10 minutes. Drain upside down.
2. Mix together bread crumbs, 1 clove garlic, thinly sliced, cheese, 1 teaspoon chopped parsley, 1 teaspoon salt, and pepper. Set aside.
3. Spread leaves of drained artichokes open slightly. Place 3 slices garlic in each artichoke. Sprinkle bread crumb mixture between leaves and over top of artichokes. Sprinkle with chopped parsley.
4. Place artichokes close together in a 10-inch skillet so they will remain upright during cooking. Pour the boiling water in the skillet and sprinkle the artichokes with olive oil.
5. Cook, covered, about 30 minutes, or until artichoke leaves are tender.

4 servings

Cream Rolls (Cannoli)

Filling:
   2 cartons (15 ounces each) ricotta
   2 teaspoons vanilla extract
   ½ cup confectioners' sugar
   ½ cup finely chopped candied citron
   ½ cup semisweet chocolate pieces

Shells:
   3 cups all-purpose flour
   ¼ cup sugar
   1 teaspoon cinnamon
   ¼ teaspoon salt
   3 tablespoons shortening
   2 eggs, well beaten
   2 tablespoons white vinegar
   2 tablespoons cold water
   Oil or shortening for deep frying
   1 egg white, slightly beaten
   ¼ to ½ cup finely chopped blanched
      pistachio nuts
   Sifted confectioners' sugar

1. To make filling, beat cheese with vanilla extract. Add ½ cup confectioners' sugar and beat until smooth. Fold in candied citron and semisweet chocolate pieces. Chill thoroughly.
2. To make the shells, combine flour, sugar, cinnamon, and salt. Using a pastry blender, cut in shortening until pieces are the size of small peas. Stir in eggs; blend in vinegar and cold water.
3. Turn dough onto a lightly floured surface and knead until smooth and elastic (5 to 10 minutes). Wrap in waxed paper and chill 30 minutes.
4. Fill a deep saucepan a little over half full with oil. Slowly heat oil to 360°F.
5. Roll out chilled dough to ⅛ inch thick. Using a 6×4½-inch oval pattern cut from cardboard, cut ovals from dough with a pastry cutter or sharp knife.
6. Wrap dough loosely around cannoli tubes (see Note), just lapping over opposite edge. Brush overlapping edges with egg white and press together to seal.
7. Fry shells in hot oil about 8 minutes, or until golden brown, turning occasionally. Fry only a few at a time, being careful not to crowd them. Using a slotted spoon or tongs, remove from oil, and drain over pan before removing to paper towels. Cool slightly and remove tubes. Cool completely.
8. When ready to serve, fill shells with ricotta filling. Sprinkle ends of filled shells with pistachio nuts and dust shells generously with confectioners' sugar.

About 16 filled rolls

Note: Aluminum cannoli tubes or clean, unpainted wooden sticks, 6 inches long and ¾ inch in diameter, may be used.

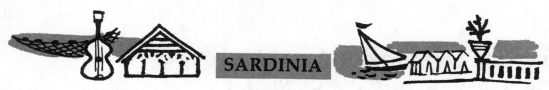

SARDINIA

A look at Sardinian cooking is like a view of an ancient city. It is archaic and relatively unspoiled by passing time. Yet, except for those few who have been lucky enough to visit the island, American familiarity with Sardinian food ends with the little fish that bears its name.

In addition to sardines, Sardinian fishermen produce a hefty haul of lobsters, tuna, swordfish, and eels from the sea. Sardinian cooks like to combine fish, hot boiled rice, and tomato sauce.

During the Roman Empire, both Sardinia and Sicily served as bread basket for the mainland; bread remains a staple in the diet of Sardinia today. One bread associated with the island is pane carasau, very thin sheets also called carta di musica, or "music paper." It is made from unleavened dough, and stacks of it have been carried into the fields by herdsmen for generations.

The wheat of Sardinia is also widely used for pasta. All of the familiar Italian pastas are found on the island, from gnocchi to spaghetti.

Today, the major agricultural pursuit of Sardinia is raising sheep; it produces about a third of Italy's total. Cattle, pigs, and goats are raised in considerable numbers, too.

With this meat supply, Sardinians have developed a cooking style based on ancient methods. For special occasions, whole suckling pigs or baby lambs are spit-roasted; smoke from juniper and olive wood imparts a unique flavor. At other times, whole animals are cooked in a hole in the ground, covered with myrtle branches.

While Sardinia is not noted for its sweets, honey-almond cakes called Sospiri are baked for holidays.

Wines are made in liberal amounts in Sardinia, and their quality is said to be good, but their names are not familiar in this country.

Rice with Lobster Sardinian Style
(Riso con Aragosta alla Sardegna)

2 large frozen lobster tails
⅔ cup minced onion
1 large clove garlic, minced
¼ cup olive oil
2 cans (16 ounces each) tomato
    purée
1 tablespoon chopped fresh basil
    leaves, or 1 teaspoon dried
    basil
1 tablespoon mild honey
1 teaspoon salt
⅛ teaspoon pepper
4 cups hot cooked rice

1. Boil lobster tails according to package directions. Cool. Remove meat from shells and cut into chunks; set aside.
2. Sauté onion and garlic in olive oil 5 minutes. Stir in tomato purée, basil, honey, salt, and pepper.
3. Simmer sauce, covered, 45 minutes. If sauce becomes too thick while it is cooking, stir in ½ cup water.
4. Combine lobster with rice, pour hot sauce over rice, and serve.

Honey-Almond Cakes (Sospiri)

2½ cups all-purpose flour
2 tablespoons baking powder
¼ teaspoon baking soda
½ teaspoon salt
½ cup butter or lard
½ cup sugar
1 egg, beaten
½ cup buckwheat honey or other
    strong honey
½ cup chopped almonds
    Cinnamon sugar (optional)

1. Combine flour, baking powder, baking soda, and salt. Cream together butter, sugar, egg, and honey. Combine with flour mixture and mix well.
2. Add almonds, knead 1 minute, and form into two 7-inch-long rolls. Wrap each roll in waxed paper and chill 2 hours. Remove dough from waxed paper, cut into ¼-inch-thick slices, and place on greased cookie sheets.
3. Bake at 350°F 10 minutes, or until lightly browned. If desired, sprinkle with cinnamon-sugar.

About 4 dozen cookies

Recipes by Category

ANTIPASTO

Suggested Foods for an Antipasto Tray

Vegetables—Marinated artichoke hearts, sliced tomatoes, sliced radishes, celery pieces, Pickled Mushrooms (page 52), Pickled Zucchini (page 52), Pickled Carrots (page 52), finocchio (fennel), green or ripe olives.

Meats—Thinly sliced meat such as salami, prosciutto, capocollo.

Eggs—Sliced hard-cooked eggs.

Fish—Sardines, tuna chunks, anchovy fillets around capers or olives.

Cheese—Slices of mozzarella, provolone, Gorgonzola

Greens—Leaf lettuce, romaine, chicory, endive.

Tomato Toast (*Crostini di Pomodori*)

¼ cup finely chopped onion
2 tablespoons butter or margarine
  Italian-style tomatoes (canned), drained
1 teaspoon sugar
⅛ teaspoon salt
1 egg yolk, fork beaten
¼ to ½ teaspoon Worcestershire sauce
¼ cup shredded Parmesan cheese
4 slices white bread, toasted, crusts removed, and toast cut in quarters
  Snipped fresh parsley or crushed dried basil or oregano

1. Add onion to heated butter in a heavy saucepan and cook until tender, stirring occasionally.
2. Force enough of the drained tomatoes through a sieve to yield 1½ cups. Add to onion with sugar and salt; cook, stirring occasionally, until liquid evaporates and mixture is thick (about 25 minutes).
3. Stir a small amount of tomato mixture into egg yolk; blend thoroughly and return to saucepan. Cook and stir 5 minutes.
4. Mix in Worcestershire sauce and half of cheese; spread generously on toast quarters. Sprinkle half of appetizers with the remaining cheese and half with the parsley.
5. Broil appetizers 3 to 4 inches from heat until bubbly. Serve hot.

16 appetizers

Pickled Zucchini (Zucchini con Olio e Aceto)

3 to 4 zucchini
5 tablespoons olive oil
2 cloves garlic, quartered
½ teaspoon oregano
¼ teaspoon salt
1 bay leaf
  Wine vinegar

1. Wash zucchini and trim off ends. Cut crosswise into ¼-inch slices.
2. Heat 3 tablespoons olive oil in a skillet. Add zucchini and cook slowly until browned. Drain on absorbent paper. Cool and put into a pint screw-top jar.
3. Combine 2 tablespoons oil, garlic, oregano, salt, and bay leaf. Pour into jar. Add enough wine vinegar to cover zucchini.
4. Store, covered, in refrigerator at least 24 hours. Serve cold.

1 pint pickle

Pickled Mushrooms (Funghi con Olio e Aceto)

1 pound fresh mushrooms (½-inch caps)
  White vinegar
  Hot water
¼ cup olive oil
2 teaspoons salt
2 teaspoons peppercorns
2 cloves garlic, quartered
1 teaspoon ground mace

1. Clean mushrooms and put into a saucepan. Pour in equal amounts of white vinegar and hot water to cover mushrooms. Bring to boiling; cook 6 minutes. Drain and cool.
2. Pack mushrooms into a pint screw-top jar and add a mixture of oil, salt, peppercorns, garlic, and mace. Add enough white vinegar to cover mushrooms.
3. Store, covered, in refrigerator 2 days. Drain and serve cold.

1 pint pickle

Italian Shrimp (Scampi Italiano)

½ cup olive or other cooking oil
¾ teaspoon salt
¼ teaspoon black pepper
½ teaspoon garlic powder
¼ cup minced parsley
1 whole pimento, mashed
2 pounds large fresh shrimp, shelled and deveined
3 tablespoons butter or margarine
3 tablespoons lemon juice

1. Mix oil, salt, pepper, garlic powder, parsley, and pimento. Dip shrimp in mixture and cook in a hot skillet over low heat about 2 minutes on each side. Spoon 2 or 3 tablespoons of the oil mixture over shrimp; cover and cook until tender (5 to 8 minutes), turning once.
2. Transfer shrimp to a serving dish. Add butter and lemon juice to the skillet; stir and heat until mixture begins to sizzle. Pour over shrimp and serve hot.

About 6 dozen shrimp

Pickled Carrots (Carote con Olio e Aceto)

6 to 8 medium carrots, pared and cut in strips
  Boiling salted water
2 tablespoons olive oil
1 clove garlic, cut in halves
1 hot green pepper
½ teaspoon salt
  Wine vinegar

1. Cook carrots in a small amount of boiling salted water in a covered saucepan until just tender. Drain and cool.
2. Pack carrots in a pint screw-top jar and add oil, garlic, hot pepper, and salt. Cover carrots with wine vinegar.
3. Store, covered, in refrigerator at least 24 hours. Drain and serve cold.

1 pint pickle

Marinated Pimentos

2 to 3 tablespoons red wine vinegar
2 cloves garlic, minced
1 bay leaf
½ teaspoon salt
½ teaspoon pepper
2 tablespoons olive or other cooking oil
2 tablespoons chili sauce
2 jars or cans (7 ounces each) whole pimentos, drained and torn in half or in large pieces
1 can anchovy fillets
¼ cup slivered ripe olives
1 tablespoon lemon juice

1. Put the vinegar, garlic, bay leaf, salt, and pepper into a saucepan; simmer 5 minutes.
2. Blend in oil and chili sauce; pour over pimentos. Let stand about 3 hours.
3. To serve, drain pimentos and garnish with anchovy fillets and ripe olives. Drizzle lemon juice over all.

About 6 servings

Eggplant Appetizer-Relish (Caponata)

¾ cup olive oil
2 cloves garlic, crushed or minced
1 large eggplant, sliced, pared, and cut in small cubes (about 3 cups)
½ cup chopped green pepper
½ cup chopped onion
¼ cup finely chopped parsley
1 tablespoon sugar
½ teaspoon crushed oregano
¼ teaspoon crushed basil
1 teaspoon seasoned salt
Few grains black pepper
1 cup canned tomato paste
¼ cup water
3 tablespoons red wine vinegar
1 can (4 ounces) mushroom stems and pieces (do not drain)
½ cup very small pimento-stuffed olives

1. Heat the oil and garlic in a large, heavy skillet. Add the eggplant, green pepper, onion, and parsley; toss to mix. Cover tightly and cook over low heat about 10 minutes.
2. Meanwhile, blend sugar, oregano, basil, salt, and pepper. Add tomato paste, water, and wine vinegar; mix well. Add to mixture in skillet and stir in remaining ingredients. Cover and cook gently until eggplant is just tender (not mushy).
3. Turn into a bowl and store, covered, in refrigerator overnight to allow flavors to blend.
4. Serve with **crackers.**

About 4 cups relish

Rosy Sauce (Salsa Rosata)

From Antico Martini, a famous restaurant on St. Mark's Square in Venice, comes this delightfully smooth and piquant dressing for seafood.

¾ cup ketchup
½ cup mayonnaise
½ cup whipping cream
2 tablespoons cognac
1½ teaspoons Worcestershire sauce
1 teaspoon prepared horseradish
4 drops Tabasco

1. Mix all ingredients; chill thoroughly.
2. Arrange chilled **cooked seafood** on **lettuce,** drizzle with **lemon juice** and spoon on sauce.

About 1½ cups sauce

George's Greek-Style Artichokes
(Carciofi alla Greca George's)

6 artichokes
4 ounces fresh mushrooms, sliced
⅔ cup coarsely chopped onion
½ cup olive oil
½ cup dry white wine
  Juice of 1 lemon
30 fennel seeds
¼ teaspoon coriander
  Salt and pepper to taste

1. Rinse artichokes and discard the hard outer leaves. Quarter artichokes, remove and discard "choke" or fuzzy part, and arrange the pieces in a large baking pan or shallow heat-resistant casserole having a cover. Allow plenty of space for the artichokes.
2. Cover artichoke pieces with the mushrooms and onion. Then pour over them a mixture of oil, wine, lemon juice, and dry seasonings.
3. Cover and place over medium heat. Bring to a rapid boil and cook about 1 minute.
4. Set in a 350°F oven about 30 minutes, or until artichokes are tender.
5. Remove from oven; cool at room temperature, then refrigerate to chill thoroughly. Serve cold.

About 8 servings

SOUPS

Escarole Soup

3 pounds beef shank cross cuts
1 can (6 ounces) tomato paste
1 tablespoon salt
1 teaspoon basil, crushed
½ teaspoon oregano, crushed
8 cups water
1 pound escarole, chopped
1 medium onion, peeled and diced
1 medium potato, pared and diced
2 stalks celery, diced
  Fresh parsley, snipped
  Freshly ground black pepper

1. Put beef shank into a saucepot or Dutch oven. Add tomato paste, salt, basil, oregano, and water; stir. Cover; bring to boiling, reduce heat, and simmer until meat is tender (about 3 hours).
2. Add escarole, onion, potato, and celery; stir. Bring to boiling; simmer, uncovered, 45 minutes, or until vegetables are tender.
3. Remove meat and bone; cut meat into pieces and transfer to soup plates. Ladle hot soup over meat and garnish each serving with parsley and pepper.

About 3 quarts soup

Vegetable Soup Italienne (Minestrone)

1 cup thinly sliced carrots
1 cup thinly sliced zucchini
1 cup thinly sliced celery
1 cup finely shredded cabbage
2 tablespoons butter
2 tablespoons cooking oil
2 beef bouillon cubes
8 cups boiling water
2 teaspoons salt
2 medium tomatoes, cut in pieces
½ cup uncooked broken spaghetti
½ teaspoon thyme

1. Add carrots, zucchini, celery, and cabbage to hot butter and oil in a saucepot. Cook, uncovered, about 10 minutes, stirring occasionally.
2. Add bouillon cubes, water, and salt to the vegetables. Bring to boiling; reduce heat and simmer, uncovered, 30 minutes.
3. Stir in tomatoes, spaghetti, and thyme; cook 20 minutes longer.
4. Serve hot from soup tureen with shredded Parmesan cheese sprinkled over the top of each serving.

About 6 servings

Chicken Broth *(Brodo di Pollo)*

1 stewing chicken (4 to 5 pounds)
5 cups water
2 teaspoons salt
5 pieces (3 inches each) celery with
    leaves
3 small carrots, washed and scraped
2 medium onions
1 large tomato, rinsed and
    quartered

1. Clean chicken, disjoint, cut into pieces, and rinse. Put into a saucepot. Rinse giblets, refrigerate liver, and put remaining giblets into pot. Add water, salt, celery, carrots, onions, and tomato. Cover and bring to boiling. Uncover and skim off foam.
2. Cover tightly. Simmer 2 to 3 hours. When chicken is almost tender, add liver. Cook about 15 minutes.
3. Remove chicken and giblets from broth, cool slightly, and remove skin. Remove meat from bones, and use as needed in recipes.
4. Strain broth and cool slightly. Remove fat that rises to surface. Refrigerate fat; use as needed. Cool broth and refrigerate until needed.

About 1 quart broth

Specialty Soup *(Zuppa Specialita)*

6 cups canned chicken broth
2 tablespoons minced parsley
2 tablespoons flour
3 eggs, well beaten
3 tablespoons shredded Parmesan
    cheese

1. Heat broth to boiling in a large saucepan.
2. Meanwhile, add parsley and flour to beaten eggs; stir in cheese and blend thoroughly.
3. Gradually add the egg mixture to boiling broth; while stirring with a fork. Cook over low heat several minutes, or until egg mixture is set.

About 6 servings

Miniatures Florentine

Float these vivid green cutouts on individual servings of hot bouillon or consommé.

1 egg, well beaten
¼ cup finely chopped fresh
    spinach
1 tablespoon finely chopped
    unblanched almonds
¼ clove garlic, minced
⅛ teaspoon salt
    Few grains black pepper

1. Mix all ingredients thoroughly in a bowl.
2. Meanwhile, heat a griddle or heavy skillet until moderately hot.
3. Lightly butter the griddle. Spoon the batter onto it, spreading to make a round about 7 inches in diameter. Bake until lightly browned, about 3 minutes; turn and brown second side.
4. Using hors d'oeuvre cutters (½ inch in diameter), cut out shapes from the griddlecake. Serve a spoonful in each serving of **soup.**

Zuppa Pavese

1 quart Chicken Broth (page 55)
4 slices bread (½ inch thick),
    toasted and generously
    buttered
4 eggs
¼ cup freshly grated Parmesan
    cheese

1. Heat Chicken Broth.
2. Place slices of buttered toast in individual heat-resistant soup bowls. Break an egg over each toast slice. Carefully pour broth into bowls, taking care not to break the egg yolks.
3. Set bowls in a 350°F oven and cook until egg whites are firm.
4. Before serving, sprinkle generously with grated cheese.

4 servings

Note: Instead of toasting and buttering the bread, the slices may be browned on both sides in butter in a skillet or on a griddle. If desired, use poached eggs and omit oven cooking.

To poach eggs, grease the bottom of a deep skillet. Add enough water to come about 1 inch above eggs. Lightly salt the water; bring to boiling, then reduce heat to simmering. Break the eggs, one at a time, into a small dish and slip each into the water. Cook 3 to 5 minutes, depending on firmness desired. Remove with slotted spoon.

BREADS

Italian Bread (Pane)

1 package active dry yeast
2 cups warm water
1 tablespoon salt
5 to 5½ cups sifted all-purpose flour

1. Soften yeast in ¼ cup warm water. Set aside.
2. Combine remaining 1¾ cups warm water and salt in a large bowl. Blend in 3 cups flour. Stir softened yeast and add to flour mixture, mixing well.
3. Add about half the remaining flour to the yeast mixture and beat until very smooth. Mix in enough remaining flour to make a soft dough. Turn dough onto lightly floured surface. Allow to rest 5 to 10 minutes. Knead 5 to 8 minutes, until dough is smooth and elastic.
4. Shape dough into a smooth ball and place in a greased bowl, just large enough to allow dough to double. Turn dough to bring greased surface to the top. Cover bowl with waxed paper and a towel. Let stand in warm place (about 80°F) until dough is doubled (1½ to 2 hours).
5. When dough has doubled in bulk, punch down with fist. Knead on a lightly floured surface about 2 minutes. Divide into 2 equal balls. Cover with towel and let stand 10 minutes.
6. Roll each ball into a 14×8-inch rectangle. Roll up lightly from wide side into a long, slender loaf. Pinch ends to seal. Place loaves on a lightly greased 15×10-inch baking sheet. Cover loaves loosely with a towel and set aside in a warm place until doubled.

7. Bake at 425°F 10 minutes. Turn oven control to 350°F and bake 1 hour, or until golden brown.

2 loaves

Note: To increase crustiness, place shallow pan on the bottom of the oven and fill with boiling water at the beginning of the baking time.

Italian Bread Sticks: Follow recipe for Italian Bread. Decrease the salt to 2 teaspoons. Lightly roll dough into rectangles ¼ inch thick and about 6 inches wide. Cut dough crosswise with a floured knife into 1-inch wide strips. With palms of hands, roll strips to pencil thickness, stretching to about 7 inches. Place strips 1 inch apart on 3 or 4 greased baking sheets. Beat **1 egg** slightly and combine with **1 tablespoon milk.** Brush the dough strips with the egg mixture. Let rise in a warm place until doubled (about 1 hour). Brush again with egg mixture and sprinkle with **coarse salt.** Bake at 400°F 18 to 20 minutes, or until sticks are browned and crisp.

About 4 dozen bread sticks

Easter Egg Bread (*Pane di Pasqua all' Uovo*)

2 packages active dry yeast
½ cup warm water
1 cup all-purpose flour
⅓ cup water
¾ cup butter or margarine
1 tablespoon grated lemon peel
1½ tablespoons lemon juice
¾ cup sugar
1 teaspoon salt
2 eggs, well beaten
3¾ to 4¼ cups all-purpose flour
6 colored eggs (uncooked)

1. Soften yeast in the warm water in a bowl. Mix in the 1 cup flour, then the ⅓ cup water. Beat until smooth. Cover; let rise in a warm place until doubled (about 1 hour).
2. Cream butter with lemon peel and juice. Add beaten eggs in halves, beating thoroughly after each addition.
3. Add yeast mixture and beat until blended. Add about half of the remaining flour and beat thoroughly. Beat in enough flour to make a soft dough.
4. Knead on floured surface until smooth. Put into a greased deep bowl; turn dough to bring greased surface to top, Cover; let rise in a warm place until doubled.
5. Punch down dough; divide into thirds. Cover; let rest about 10 minutes.
6. With hands, roll and stretch each piece into a roll about 26 inches long and ¾ inch thick. Loosely braid rolls together. On a lightly greased baking sheet or jelly-roll pan shape into a ring, pressing ends together. At even intervals, gently spread dough apart and tuck in a colored egg. Cover; let rise again until doubled.
7. Bake at 375°F about 30 minutes. During baking check bread for browning, and when sufficiently browned, cover loosely with aluminum foil.
8. Transfer coffee cake to a wire rack. If desired, spread a confectioners' sugar icing over top of warm bread.

1 large wreath

Tomato-Cheese Pizza
(Pizza al Formaggio e Pomodoro)

½ package active dry yeast
1 cup plus 2 tablespoons warm
    water
4 cups sifted all-purpose flour
1 teaspoon salt
3 cups drained canned tomatoes
8 ounces mozzarella cheese, thinly
    sliced
½ cup olive oil
¼ cup grated Parmesan cheese
1 teaspoon salt
½ teaspoon pepper
2 teaspoons oregano

1. Soften yeast in 2 tablespoons warm water. Set aside.
2. Pour remaining cup of warm water into a large bowl. Blend in 2 cups flour and 1 teaspoon salt. Stir softened yeast and add to flour-water mixture, mixing well.
3. Add about 1 cup flour to yeast mixture and beat until very smooth. Mix in enough remaining flour to make a soft dough. Turn dough onto a lightly floured surface and allow to rest 5 to 10 minutes. Knead 5 to 8 minutes, until dough is smooth and elastic.
4. Shape dough into a smooth ball and place in a greased bowl just large enough to allow dough to double. Turn dough to bring greased surface to top. Cover with waxed paper and let stand in warm place (about 80°F) until dough is doubled (about 1½ to 2 hours).
5. Punch down with fist. Fold edge towards center and turn dough over. Divide dough into two equal balls. Grease another bowl and place one of the balls in it. Turn dough in both bowls so greased side is on top. Cover and let rise again until almost doubled (about 45 minutes).
6. Roll each ball of dough into a 14×10-inch rectangle, ⅛ inch thick. Place on two lightly greased 15½×12-inch baking sheets. Shape edges by pressing dough between thumb and forefinger to make a ridge. If desired, dough may be rolled into rounds, ⅛ inch thick.
7. Force tomatoes through a sieve or food mill and spread 1½ cups on each pizza. Arrange 4 ounces of mozzarella cheese on each pizza. Sprinkle over each pizza, in the order given, ¼ cup olive oil, 2 tablespoons grated Parmesan cheese, ½ teaspoon salt, ¼ teaspoon pepper, and 1 teaspoon oregano.
8. Bake at 400°F 25 to 30 minutes, or until crust is browned. Cut into wedges to serve.

6 to 8 servings

Mushroom Pizza: Follow Tomato-Cheese Pizza recipe. Before baking, place on each pizza 1 cup (8-ounce can) drained **button mushrooms.**

Sausage Pizza: Follow Tomato-Cheese Pizza recipe. Before baking, place on each pizza 1 pound **hot Italian sausage** (with casing removed), cut in ¼-inch pieces.

Anchovy Pizza: Follow Tomato-Cheese Pizza recipe. Omit mozzarella and Parmesan cheeses, decrease amount of oregano to ¼ teaspoon, and top each pizza with 8 **anchovy fillets,** cut in ¼-inch pieces.

Miniature Pizza: Follow Tomato-Cheese Pizza recipe. After rolling dough, cut dough into 3½-inch rounds. Shape edge of rounds as in Tomato-Cheese Pizza recipe. Using half the amount of ingredients in that recipe, spread each pizza with 2 tablespoons sieved canned tomatoes. Top with a slice of mozzarella cheese. Sprinkle cheese with ½ teaspoon olive

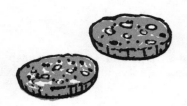

oil, ½ teaspoon grated Parmesan cheese, and a few grains salt and pepper. Bake at 400°F 15 to 20 minutes, or until crust is browned.

About 24 miniature pizzas

English Muffin Pizza: Split 12 **English muffins** and spread cut sides with **butter or margarine.** Toast under the broiler until lightly browned. Top each half as for Miniature Pizza. Bake at 400°F 5 to 8 minutes, or until tomato mixture is bubbling hot.

PASTA AND RICE

Basic Noodle Dough (Pasta)

4 **cups sifted all-purpose flour**
½ **teaspoon salt**
4 **eggs**
6 **tablespoons cold water**

1. Mix flour and salt in a bowl; make a well in center. Add eggs, one at a time, mixing slightly after each addition. Add water gradually, mixing to make a stiff dough.
2. Turn dough onto a lightly floured surface and knead until smooth.
3. Proceed as directed in recipes.

Lasagnette

Tomato Meat Sauce (half recipe, page 84)
Basic Noodle Dough
8 **quarts water**
¼ **cup salt**
1 **tablespoon olive oil**
1 **cup (8 ounces) ricotta**
2 **tablespoons grated Parmesan cheese**
¼ **teaspoon salt**
⅛ **teaspoon pepper**

1. Prepare Tomato Meat Sauce.
2. Prepare noodle dough. Roll lightly ⅛ inch thick to form a rectangle about 12 inches long. Cut dough lengthwise with pastry cutter into strips ½ to ¾ inch wide.
3. Bring water to boiling in a large saucepot. Add ¼ cup salt, then noodles. Boil rapidly, uncovered, about 15 minutes, or until tender. Drain by pouring into a colander or large sieve; keep warm.
4. Put ½ cup meat sauce into a saucepan. Mix in ricotta, Parmesan cheese, ¼ teaspoon salt, and pepper. Cook over low heat until thoroughly heated.
5. Put noodles on a warm serving platter and pour cheese sauce over them. Cover with meat sauce. Serve immediately.

About 8 servings

Lasagne II

Tomato Sauce with Meat (page 82)
1 **pound lasagne noodles, cooked, drained, and rinsed**
2 **pounds ricotta**
1 **pound mozzarella or scamorze cheese, shredded**
1 **cup shredded Parmesan cheese**

1. Prepare Tomato Sauce with Meat.
2. Spread about 1 cup tomato sauce in a buttered 13×9×2-inch baking dish. Using a fourth of each, add a layer of noodles and then one of tomato sauce. Using a third of each, top evenly with 3 cheeses. Repeat layering and end with sauce.
3. Heat in a 375°F oven about 30 minutes, or until bubbly. Allow to stand 10 to 15 minutes to set layers before serving. Cut into squares.

12 to 15 servings

Shells with Clam Sauce
(Conchiglie con Salsa alle Vongole)

4 quarts water
1 tablespoon salt
2 cups (8-ounce package) macaroni
    shells
   White Clam Sauce (page 43)
1 tablespoon minced parsley

1. Bring water to boiling in a large saucepan or saucepot. Add salt, then macaroni. Boil rapidly, uncovered, 10 to 12 minutes, or until tender.
2. Meanwhile, prepare clam sauce.
3. Drain macaroni and put into a warm serving bowl. Pour clam sauce over macaroni and sprinkle with parsley.

4 to 6 servings

Macaroni Muffs (Manicotti)

   Tomato Meat Sauce (page 84)
2 tablespoons olive oil
½ pound ground beef
2 cups (about 1 pound) ricotta
¼ pound mozzarella cheese, diced
2 teaspoons grated Parmesan
    cheese
2 eggs, well beaten
¾ teaspoon salt
¼ teaspoon pepper
   Basic Noodle Dough (one-half
    recipe, page 59)
5 quarts water
1 tablespoon salt

1. Prepare Tomato Meat Sauce.
2. While sauce is cooking, heat oil in a skillet. Add ground beef and cook until no pink color remains.
3. Combine cheeses, eggs, ¾ teaspoon salt, and pepper. Mix in meat. Set aside.
4. Prepare noodle dough. Divide dough into halves. Lightly roll each half ⅛ inch thick to form a rectangle. Cut dough lengthwise with pastry cutter into strips 5 inches wide. Cut strips every 6 inches to form noodles 5×6 inches.
5. Bring water to boiling in a large saucepot. Add 1 tablespoon salt, then noodles. Boil rapidly, uncovered, 10 to 12 minutes, or until noodles are tender. Drain.
6. Lay noodles out flat on a working surface. About ½ inch from the lengthwise edge of the noodle, put 4 tablespoons filling. Spread filling from narrow edge to narrow edge so filling is in a ½-inch-wide mound. Roll the ½-inch edge of the dough over filling and continue to roll. Press edges to seal. Put 4 to 6 manicotti into each of two 11×7×1½-inch baking dishes in a single layer. Cover with sauce.
7. Bake at 400°F 15 to 20 minutes, or until tomato sauce is bubbly hot. Serve with remaining sauce.

8 to 12 manicotti

Mostaccioli and Cheese (Mostaccioli al Formaggio)

   Tomato Meat Sauce (page 84)
4 quarts water
1 tablespoon salt
2 cups (8-ounce package)
    mostaccioli
1 cup chopped mozzarella cheese
2 tablespoons grated Parmesan
    cheese
¼ teaspoon pepper
   Grated Parmesan or Romano
    cheese

1. Prepare Tomato Meat Sauce.
2. Heat water to boiling in a large saucepan. Add salt, then mostaccioli. Boil rapidly, uncovered, 12 to 15 minutes, or until tender. Drain.
3. Returned drained mostaccioli to saucepan and mix in 2 tablespoons meat sauce. Turn half of mostaccioli into an 8-inch square baking dish. Add cheeses and pepper in layers, then the remaining mostaccioli. Cover with additional meat sauce.
4. Bake at 350°F 15 to 20 minutes, or until sauce is bubbling.
5. Serve with remaining meat sauce. Sprinkle with grated cheese.

4 to 6 servings

Green Noodles in Pastry
(Tagliatelle Verdi Pasticciate)

1 unbaked deep 9-inch pie shell
6 large mushrooms, cleaned and sliced
2 tablespoons butter
12 ounces green noodles
1 tablespoon butter
¼ cup grated Parmesan cheese
1 cup Bolognese Meat Sauce (page 85)
1½ cups Cream Sauce (page 26)
1 mushroom cap
6 to 8 mushroom halves
1 tablespoon butter, melted
Grated Parmesan cheese

1. Thoroughly prick bottom and sides of pie shell. Bake at 450°F about 7 minutes, or until lightly browned; set aside.
2. Sauté mushrooms in 2 tablespoons butter 3 minutes. Cook noodles according to package directions and drain.
3. Combine noodles, mushrooms, 1 tablespoon butter, ¼ cup cheese, meat sauce, and 1 cup Cream Sauce. Turn mixture into pie shell. Spread remaining ½ cup Cream Sauce over top. Put mushroom cap in center and surround with mushroom halves. Drizzle melted butter over all and sprinkle with additional cheese.
4. Bake at 400°F about 8 minutes, or until heated through and top is slightly browned.

About 6 servings

Green Noodles *(Pasta Verde)*

¼ pound spinach
3 cups sifted all-purpose flour
½ teaspoon salt
3 eggs
6 quarts water
1 tablespoon salt
¾ cup grated Parmesan cheese
½ teaspoon salt
¼ cup butter

1. Wash spinach and put into a heavy saucepan. Do not add water; cook only in moisture remaining on leaves from washing. Partially cover and cook 5 minutes, stirring occasionally with a fork.
2. Drain spinach, pressing out water, and chop finely.
3. Mix flour and ½ teaspoon salt in a bowl; make a well in center. Add eggs, one at a time, mixing slightly after each addition. Add the chopped spinach and mix well.
4. Turn dough onto a lightly floured surface and knead until smooth, adding flour if needed for a stiff dough.
5. Divide dough in half. Lightly roll each half into a rectangle, about ⅛ inch thick. Cover; let stand 1 hour. Beginning with a narrow end, gently fold over about 2 inches of dough and continue folding over so final width is about 3 inches. (Dough must be dry enough so layers do not stick together.) Beginning at a narrow edge, cut dough into strips ¼ inch wide. Unroll strips and arrange on waxed paper on a flat surface. Let stand until noodles are dry (2 to 3 hours).
6. Bring water to boiling in a large saucepot. Add 1 tablespoon salt. Add noodles gradually. Boil rapidly, uncovered, 8 to 10 minutes, or until tender.
7. Drain noodles and put a third of them into a greased 2-quart casserole. Top with a third each of the cheese and remaining salt. Dot with a third of butter. Repeat layering twice.
8. Bake at 350°F 15 to 20 minutes, or until cheese is melted.

About 8 servings

Ravioli

Tomato Meat Sauce (page 84)
3 cups (about 1½ pounds) ricotta
1½ tablespoons chopped parsley
2 eggs, well beaten
1 tablespoon grated Parmesan
  cheese
¾ teaspoon salt
¼ teaspoon pepper
  Basic Noodle Dough (page 59)
7 quarts water
2 tablespoons salt
  Grated Parmesan or Romano
  cheese

1. Prepare Tomato Meat Sauce.
2. Mix ricotta, parsley, eggs, 1 tablespoon grated Parmesan, ¾ teaspoon salt, and pepper.
3. Prepare noodle dough. Divide dough in fourths. Lightly roll each fourth ⅛ inch thick to form a rectangle. Cut dough lengthwise with pastry cutter into strips 5 inches wide. Put 2 teaspoons filling 1½ inches from narrow end in center of each strip. Continuing along strip, put 2 teaspoons filling at 3½-inch intervals.
4. Fold each strip in half lengthwise, covering mounds of filling. To seal, press the edges together with the tines of a fork. Press gently between mounds to form rectangles about 3½ inches long. Cut apart with a pastry cutter and press cut edges of rectangles with tines of fork to seal.
5. Bring water to boiling in a large saucepot. Add 2 tablespoons salt. Add ravioli gradually; cook about half of ravioli at one time. Boil, uncovered, about 20 minutes, or until tender. Remove with slotted spoon and drain. Put on a warm platter and top with Tomato Meat Sauce. Sprinkle with grated cheese.

About 3 dozen ravioli

Ravioli with Meat Filling: Follow recipe for Ravioli. Prepare sauce. Omit ricotta and parsley. Heat **2 tablespoons olive oil** in a skillet. Add **¾ pound ground beef** and cook until no pink color remains. Cook **½ pound spinach** until tender (see step 1 of Green Noodles, page 61); drain. Mix spinach and ground beef with egg mixture. Proceed as directed.

Seafood-Sauced Green Noodles

1½ pounds medium-size fresh
  shrimp
3 tablespoons olive oil
2 tablespoons lemon juice
1 clove garlic, minced
2 tablespoons butter
  Clam Sauce (page 82)
8 ounces green noodles (packaged
  or homemade), cooked and
  drained

1. Shell and devein shrimp; rinse under running cold water and drain.
2. Mix olive oil, lemon juice, and garlic in a bowl. Add shrimp; cover and marinate about 2 hours, tossing occasionally. Remove shrimp; set marinade aside.
3. Add shrimp to hot butter in a skillet; cook, turning frequently, until pink and tender, about 10 minutes.
4. Remove shrimp with a slotted spoon. Cut about two thirds of shrimp into pieces; reserve remainder. Blend pieces into Clam Sauce; keep warm.
5. Add reserved marinade to skillet; heat. Toss cooked noodles with hot marinade; turn into a heated serving dish. Pour sauce over noodles, sprinkle with **grated Romano cheese,** and garnish with whole shrimp.

About 6 servings

Macaroni alla Savonarola

½ pound ground veal
¾ cup fine dry bread crumbs
1 egg, beaten
2 tablespoons shredded Parmesan cheese
¼ teaspoon ground nutmeg
¼ teaspoon salt
1 cup uncooked green peas, fresh or frozen
2 tablespoons butter
⅓ cup finely chopped onion
1 cup finely chopped cooked ham
3 tablespoons butter
3 hard-cooked eggs, cut in ¼-inch cubes
2 cups whipping cream
1 pound maccaroncini (big spaghetti with a hole), cooked and drained
½ cup shredded Parmesan cheese

1. Mix half of the ground veal with bread crumbs, egg, 2 tablespoons cheese, nutmeg, and salt to make a smooth mixture. Form into small balls.
2. In a large ovenware skillet, cook peas in 2 tablespoons hot butter until lightly browned. Add the meatballs to the skillet. Set in a 375°F oven for 20 minutes.
3. Lightly brown onion, ham, and remaining veal in 3 tablespoons butter in a saucepan.
4. Add the ham-veal mixture, hard-cooked eggs, and cream to the skillet; mix well. Bring to boiling; simmer about 15 minutes.
5. Turn maccaroncini onto a platter, pour sauce over it, and sprinkle remaining Parmesan cheese over all.

6 to 8 servings

Spaghetti with Meatballs (Spaghetti con Polpette)

Tomato Meat Sauce (page 84)
½ pound ground beef
½ pound ground pork
1 cup soft bread crumbs
1 tablespoon grated Parmesan cheese
1 tablespoon minced parsley
1 egg, well beaten
1 teaspoon salt
¼ teaspoon pepper
2 tablespoons olive oil
1 clove garlic, minced
4 quarts water
1 tablespoon salt
8 ounces long spaghetti
Grated Parmesan or Romano cheese

1. Prepare Tomato Meat Sauce.
2. While sauce is cooking, lightly mix ground meat with bread crumbs, 1 tablespoon Parmesan cheese, parsley, egg, 1 teaspoon salt, and pepper. Shape mixture into balls about 1 inch in diameter.
3. Heat oil and garlic in a skillet. Add meatballs and brown on all sides. Add meatballs to sauce about 20 minutes before sauce is cooked.
4. Heat water to boiling in a saucepot. Add 1 tablespoon salt. Add spaghetti and stir with a fork. Boil rapidly, uncovered, 10 to 12 minutes, or until tender. Drain.
5. Put spaghetti on a warm platter and top with sauce. Sprinkle with grated cheese.

4 to 6 servings

Spaghetti with Wine Tomato Sauce: Follow recipe for Spaghetti with Meatballs. About 30 minutes before sauce is done, add **½ cup dry red wine.**

Spaghetti with Tomato Sauce: Follow recipe for Spaghetti with Meatballs. Omit meatballs. Top spaghetti with Tomato Meat Sauce or a variation.

Pasta with Broccoli *(Pasta e Broccoli)*

4 quarts water
2 teaspoons salt
4 cups (1-pound package) ditalini
1 pound broccoli, washed and
    trimmed
¼ cup olive oil
2 cloves garlic, sliced
⅛ teaspoon pepper
Grated Parmesan or Romano
    cheese

1. Heat water to boiling in a large saucepan. Add salt, then ditalini. Boil rapidly, uncovered, about 12 minutes, or until tender. Drain, reserving 3 cups liquid. Set aside.
2. Put broccoli into a small amount of boiling salted water. Cook uncovered 5 minutes, then cover and cook 10 to 15 minutes, or until just tender. Drain if necessary and keep warm.
3. Heat oil and garlic in a large saucepan until garlic is lightly browned.
4. Add broccoli and ditalini with the reserved cooking liquid. Season with pepper. Simmer about 10 minutes.
5. Top with grated cheese and serve immediately.

About 6 servings

Pasta with Peas *(Pasta e Piselli)*

2 quarts water
1 teaspoon salt
2 cups (8-ounce package) ditalini
¼ cup olive oil
¼ cup chopped onion
½ cup canned tomatoes, sieved
¾ teaspoon salt
⅛ teaspoon pepper
⅛ teaspoon oregano
2 cans (16 ounces each) green peas,
    drained
Grated Parmesan or Romano
    cheese

1. Heat water to boiling in a large saucepan. Add 1 teaspoon salt, then ditalini. Boil rapidly, uncovered, about 12 minutes, or until tender. Drain, reserving 2 cups liquid.
2. Heat oil in a large saucepan. Add onion and cook until lightly browned. Add tomatoes, ¾ teaspoon salt, pepper, and oregano; mix well. Simmer about 10 minutes.
3. Add cooked ditalini, reserved cooking liquid, and drained peas. Simmer about 10 minutes.
4. Top with grated cheese and serve immediately.

4 to 6 servings

Pasta with Beans *(Pasta e Fagioli)*

3 cups water
1¼ cups (about ½ pound) dried
    navy beans, rinsed
½ teaspoon salt
2 quarts water
1 teaspoon salt

1. Heat 3 cups water to boiling in a large saucepan. Add beans gradually to water. Boil 2 minutes. Remove from heat and cover, and set aside 1 hour.
2. Add ½ teaspoon salt to soaked beans. Bring to boiling, reduce heat, and simmer, covered, 2 hours, or until beans are tender; stir once or twice.

Baked Rice Balls, 48, from Sicily

2 cups (8-ounce package) ditalini
¼ cup canned tomatoes, sieved
1 tablespoon olive oil
¼ teaspoon pepper
¼ teaspoon oregano
   Grated Parmesan cheese

3. Meanwhile, heat 2 quarts water to boiling in a large saucepan. Add 1 teaspoon salt, then ditalini. Boil rapidly, uncovered, about 12 minutes, or until ditalini is tender. Drain, reserving 1 cup liquid.
4. When beans are tender, add the drained ditalini, the 1 cup reserved liquid, tomatoes, oil, pepper, and oregano. Simmer 10 to 15 minutes.
5. Sprinkle with grated cheese and serve immediately.

About 6 servings

Lemon Rice with Egg *(Riso all' Uovo e Limone)*

1¾ cups chicken broth
¾ cup uncooked long grain rice
1 egg
1 tablespoon lemon juice
¼ cup grated Parmesan cheese

1. Bring broth to boiling in a saucepan. Stir in rice; cover tightly. Cook 15 to 20 minutes, or until rice is tender and liquid is absorbed.
2. Place egg, lemon juice, and cheese in a bowl; beat until foamy. Stir into rice over low heat. Serve immediately.

About 4 servings

Gnocchi alla Semolino

1 quart milk
1 teaspoon salt
⅛ teaspoon freshly ground nutmeg
1 cup uncooked farina or semolina
¼ cup butter
3 eggs, well beaten
½ cup freshly shredded Parmesan cheese
   Butter
   Freshly shredded Parmesan cheese

1. Put milk, salt, and nutmeg into a heavy saucepan and bring to boiling. Add farina gradually, stirring constantly to prevent lumping. Cook and stir over low heat 10 minutes, or until very thick.
2. Remove from heat and beat in ¼ cup butter, eggs, and ½ cup cheese. Spread mixture about ½ inch thick on a greased baking sheet with sides. Chill thoroughly.
3. When ready to bake, top with bits of butter and a generous sprinkling of Parmesan cheese.
4. Heat in a 425°F oven until top is browned.
5. To serve, cut into squares.

About 8 servings

MEAT, POULTRY, AND SEAFOOD

Hunter-Style Lamb with Fettuccine
(Agnello Cacciatore con Fettuccine)

2 pounds lamb (leg, loin, or shoulder), trimmed and cut in 1½-inch cubes
¾ to 1 teaspoon salt
¼ to ½ teaspoon pepper
2 tablespoons butter
2 tablespoons olive oil
4 anchovies, chopped
1 clove garlic, minced
1 medium green pepper, cleaned and cut in pieces
Olive oil
1 teaspoon rosemary, crushed
1 teaspoon basil, crushed
¼ teaspoon sage, crushed
½ cup red wine vinegar
Chicken broth
2 teaspoons flour
8 ounces fettuccine noodles, cooked and drained
Grated Parmesan cheese
Minced parsley

1. Season lamb with salt and pepper.
2. Heat butter and 2 tablespoons oil in a large, heavy skillet; add meat and brown on all sides.
3. Meanwhile, cook anchovies, garlic, and green pepper in a small amount of oil in a small saucepan about 5 minutes. Add rosemary, basil, sage, and vinegar; mix well. Cook and stir until boiling.
4. Remove lamb from skillet with a slotted spoon; set aside. Add enough chicken broth to drippings in skillet to make ¾ cup liquid. Add herb-vinegar mixture and bring to boiling, stirring to blend. Return lamb to skillet, cover tightly, and simmer over low heat about 40 minutes, or until tender.
5. Combine flour with a small amount of water to make a smooth paste. Add to liquid in skillet; cook and stir until mixture comes to boiling; cook 1 to 2 minutes.
6. Serve on a heated serving platter surrounded with fettuccine tossed with grated Parmesan cheese. Sprinkle with parsley.

About 6 servings

Roast Leg of Lamb, Italian Style
(Cosciotto d'Agnello alla Italiano)

1 lamb leg (5 to 6 pounds); do not remove fell
Garlic cloves, cut in slivers
⅓ cup olive oil
1 tablespoon grated lemon peel
1½ teaspoons salt
¼ teaspoon pepper
1 teaspoon rosemary

1. Cut several small slits in surface of meat and insert a sliver of garlic in each.
2. Place lamb, skin side down, on rack in a roasting pan. Brush meat with olive oil. Sprinkle with lemon peel and a mixture of salt, pepper, and rosemary. Insert meat thermometer so tip is slightly beyond center of thickest part of meat; be sure that it does not rest in fat or on bone.
3. Roast, uncovered, at 325°F 2 to 3¼ hours, allowing 25 to 35 minutes per pound. Meat is medium done when thermometer registers 160°F and is well done at 170°F-180°F.
4. Remove meat to a warm serving platter. Garnish with parsley sprigs, if desired.

8 to 10 servings

Veal Chops Pizzaiola *(Scaloppine alla Pizzaiola)*

¼ cup olive oil
6 veal rib or loin chops, cut about
  ½ inch thick
1 can (28 ounces) tomatoes, sieved
2 cloves garlic, sliced
1 teaspoon oregano
1 teaspoon salt
½ teaspoon pepper
½ teaspoon chopped parsley

1. Heat oil in a large, heavy skillet. Add chops and brown on both sides.
2. Meanwhile, combine tomatoes, garlic, oregano, salt, pepper, and parsley. Slowly add tomato mixture to browned veal. Cover and cook over low heat 45 minutes, or until meat is tender.

6 servings

Beefsteak Pizzaiola: Follow recipe for Veal Chops Pizzaiola. Substitute **2 pounds beef round steak,** cut about ¾ inch thick, for veal chops. Cook about 1½ hours.

Veal Scaloppine with Mushrooms and Capers
(Scaloppine di Vitella con Funghi e Capperi)

1 pound veal round steak, cut
  about ½ inch thick
½ cup flour
½ teaspoon salt
⅛ teaspoon pepper
¼ cup olive oil
½ clove garlic, minced
¼ cup butter
½ pound mushrooms, cleaned and
  sliced lengthwise
1 medium onion, thinly sliced
1¾ cups sieved canned tomatoes
¼ cup capers
1 teaspoon salt
⅛ teaspoon pepper
¼ teaspoon minced parsley
¼ teaspoon oregano

1. Put meat on a flat working surface and pound on both sides with a meat hammer. Cut into 1-inch pieces. Coat evenly with a mixture of flour, ½ teaspoon salt, and ⅛ teaspoon pepper.
2. Heat oil with garlic in a large skillet. Add veal and slowly brown on both sides.
3. Meanwhile, heat butter in a skillet. Add mushrooms and onion; cook until mushrooms are lightly browned.
4. Add mushrooms to veal along with tomatoes, capers, 1 teaspoon salt, ⅛ teaspoon pepper, parsley, and oregano; mix well.
5. Cover skillet and simmer about 25 minutes, or until veal is tender; stir occasionally.

About 4 servings

Veal Marsala (Scaloppine di Vitella al Marsala)

1½ to 2 pounds veal round steak,
    cut about ½ inch thick
¼ cup flour
1 teaspoon salt
⅛ teaspoon pepper
1 clove garlic, thinly sliced
¼ cup olive oil
¼ cup Marsala
¼ cup water
¼ teaspoon chopped parsley
⅛ teaspoon salt
⅛ teaspoon pepper

1. Place meat on a flat working surface and pound with a meat hammer on both sides. Cut into 6 pieces.
2. Coat veal with a mixture of flour, 1 teaspoon salt, and ⅛ teaspoon pepper.
3. Heat garlic and oil in a large, heavy skillet until garlic is slightly browned. Add meat to oil and garlic in skillet; brown slowly on both sides.
4. Meanwhile, combine Marsala, water, parsley, ⅛ teaspoon salt, and ⅛ teaspoon pepper. Slowly add Marsala mixture to browned veal. Cover and cook over low heat 20 minutes, or until veal is tender.

6 servings

Veal Cannelloni

¼ cup finely chopped onion
¼ cup finely chopped celery
2 tablespoons finely chopped carrot
1 tablespoon minced parsley
2 tablespoons olive oil
2 cups ground cooked veal
¼ teaspoon salt
⅛ teaspoon white pepper
¼ teaspoon oregano, crushed
¼ teaspoon basil, crushed
½ cup strong chicken broth (1
    chicken bouillon cube
    dissolved in ½ cup boiling
    water)
⅛ teaspoon nutmeg
2 cups Medium White Sauce (page
    83)
Pasta for Cannelloni
¼ cup tomato sauce
¼ cup cream
1 cup grated Parmesan cheese

1. Cook onion, celery, carrot, and parsley in hot oil in a skillet about 3 minutes. Stir in veal, salt, pepper, oregano, basil, and chicken broth. Cook about 15 minutes.
2. Stir ½ cup white sauce into veal mixture.
3. Prepare pasta.
4. Spoon veal filling equally on the pasta squares and roll up. Arrange on an oven-proof platter.
5. Blend tomato sauce and cream into remaining white sauce; pour over cannelloni. Sprinkle top with cheese.
6. Set in a 425°F oven 10 minutes, or until top is browned.

4 servings

Pasta for Cannelloni

2 cups all-purpose flour
¼ teaspoon salt
1 egg, beaten
2 egg yolks, beaten
7 tablespoons water
4 quarts water
1 tablespoon salt

1. Blend flour and ¼ teaspoon salt in a bowl. Using a fork, stir in egg and egg yolks. Gradually add 7 tablespoons water, stirring constantly to make a stiff dough.
2. Turn dough onto a lightly floured surface and knead until smooth. Divide dough into halves and roll each into a rectangle ¹/₁₆ inch thick. Cut into eight 6×4-inch rectangles. Dry 1 hour. (Any leftover dough may be cut into strips, dried, and used as noodles.)
3. Bring 4 quarts water to boiling in a large saucepan. Add 1 tablespoon salt, then cannelloni squares. Boil, uncovered, about 8 minutes, or until just tender. Drain, rinse with cold water, and drain again.

8 cannelloni squares

Meat-and-Spinach-Filled Pancake Rolls
(Cannelloni alla Piemontese "Maison")

6 thin 10-inch pancakes*
⅓ cup finely chopped onion
3 tablespoons olive oil
½ pound ground veal, cooked (or other cooked meat)
1 package (10 ounces) frozen chopped spinach, cooked and drained
1 egg
⅓ cup grated Parmesan cheese
¼ teaspoon salt
Pinch pepper
Pinch nutmeg
1½ cups Béchamel Sauce (page 83)

1. Prepare pancakes and cut into 2½-inch squares; keep warm.
2. Cook onion in heated olive oil in a skillet about 3 minutes. Add ground meat and cook until lightly browned. Mix spinach with meat mixture; force mixture through medium blade of food chopper.
3. Mix egg, cheese, salt, pepper, and nutmeg with meat mixture until thoroughly blended. Place about 1 tablespoon meat mixture on each pancake square and roll each into a sausage shape.
4. Arrange the filled cannelloni in a shallow buttered baking dish; cover with Béchamel Sauce.
5. Heat in a 375°F oven until golden brown. Serve very hot.

4 to 6 servings

*Prepare pancakes using batter in recipe for Stuffed Pancakes (page 40).

Scamorze-Crowned Veal with Mushrooms

2 pounds veal cutlets, cut about ½ inch thick
¼ cup lemon juice
½ teaspoon salt
1/16 teaspoon black pepper
¼ cup butter
½ cup flour
1 egg, beaten
½ cup fine dry bread crumbs
¼ pound mushrooms, cleaned and sliced
6 thin slices cooked ham
6 ounces scamorze cheese, cut in 6 slices
6 mushroom caps, browned in butter

1. Cut meat into 6 serving-size pieces; place on a flat working surface and pound both sides with a meat hammer. Put into a large, shallow dish.
2. Mix lemon juice, salt, and pepper together and spoon over veal. Cover and refrigerate 2 hours.
3. Heat butter in a large, heavy skillet. Coat veal pieces with flour, dip in egg, then in bread crumbs. Add to hot butter in skillet and fry about 5 minutes on one side, or until lightly browned.
4. Turn meat and arrange on each piece a layer of mushroom slices, a slice of ham, a slice of cheese, and a mushroom cap. Continue cooking about 5 minutes, or until second side is browned and cheese is melted.
5. Remove to a warm serving platter and serve immediately.

6 servings

Veal Parmesan (Scaloppine di Vitella alla Parmigiana)

2 cups Tomato Meat Sauce (page 84)
1½ to 2 pounds veal round steak, cut about ½ inch thick
1⅓ cups fine dry bread crumbs
⅓ cup grated Parmesan cheese
3 eggs, beaten
1 teaspoon salt
¼ teaspoon pepper
⅓ cup olive oil
6 slices (3 ounces) mozzarella cheese

1. Prepare Tomato Meat Sauce.
2. Put meat on a flat working surface and repeatedly pound on one side with meat hammer. Turn meat over and repeat process. Cut into 6 pieces.
3. Mix bread crumbs and grated cheese; set aside.
4. Mix eggs, salt, and pepper; set aside.
5. Heat oil in a large skillet. Coat meat pieces first with egg, then with crumb mixture. Add to oil in skillet and brown on both sides.
6. Put browned meat into an 11×7×1½-inch baking dish. Pour sauce over meat. Top with slices of mozzarella cheese.
7. Bake at 350°F 15 to 20 minutes, or until cheese is melted and lightly browned.

6 servings

Ham-and-Asparagus-Stuffed Veal Rolls
(Manicaretti alla Lucrezia Borgia)

6 slices (1½ pounds) veal cutlet, boneless
1 teaspoon salt
¼ teaspoon black pepper
6 slices prosciutto
6 slices Emmenthaler cheese
6 white asparagus spears, 4 inches long
¼ cup butter
½ cup port wine
2 tablespoons butter
⅓ cup finely chopped parsley
2 cloves garlic, crushed
3½ ounces dried mushrooms, hydrated (soaked in water)
¼ cup beef gravy
3 cups cream
1 teaspoon salt

1. Pound veal cutlets until thin. Season with salt and pepper.
2. Place a slice of prosciutto, then a slice of cheese and an asparagus spear, over each veal slice. Roll into fingers; skewer or secure with twine.
3. Melt the ¼ cup butter in a large, heavy skillet. Add veal rolls; brown on all sides. Add port wine; cover and simmer about 10 minutes.
4. Meanwhile, melt the 2 tablespoons butter in a saucepan. Add and lightly brown the parsley and garlic. Mix in the mushrooms, beef gravy, and cream; simmer 5 minutes. Pour sauce over veal rolls; correct seasoning, using the remaining 1 teaspoon salt. Cover and simmer until meat is tender.

6 servings

Veal Rollettes (Rosolini di Vitella)

2 cloves garlic, minced
1 tablespoon grated Parmesan
    cheese
2 teaspoons chopped parsley
½ teaspoon salt
¼ teaspoon pepper
1½ pounds veal round steak, cut
    about ½ inch thick
    Mozzarella cheese, sliced
3 tablespoons olive oil
½ cup butter, melted
¼ cup water

1. Mix garlic, Parmesan cheese, parsley, salt, and pepper. Set aside.
2. Cut veal into 4×3-inch pieces. Put 1 slice mozzarella cheese on each piece of meat. Top each with 1 teaspoon garlic-cheese mixture. Roll each piece of meat to enclose mixture; tie with string, or fasten meat roll with wooden picks or small skewers.
3. Heat oil in a skillet. Add meat rolls and brown slowly on all sides. Put meat into a greased 2-quart casserole. Mix butter and water; pour over meat. Cover casserole.
4. Bake at 300°F about 1 hour, or until meat is tender. Remove string, wooden picks, or skewers.

About 4 servings

Fried Chicken (Pollo Fritto)

1 frying chicken (about 3
    pounds), cut in serving pieces
½ cup flour
1½ teaspoons salt
¼ teaspoon pepper
    Olive oil
2 eggs, well beaten
¼ cup milk
1 tablespoon chopped parsley
½ cup grated Parmesan cheese
1 to 2 tablespoons water

1. Rinse chicken and pat dry with paper towels. To coat chicken evenly, shake 2 or 3 pieces at a time in a plastic bag containing the flour, salt, and pepper.
2. Fill a large, heavy skillet ½-inch deep with olive oil; place over medium heat.
3. Combine eggs, milk, and parsley. Dip each chicken piece in the egg mixture and roll in cheese. Starting with meaty pieces, place the chicken, skin-side down, in the hot oil. Turn pieces as necessary to brown evenly on all sides.
4. When chicken is browned, reduce heat, pour in water, and cover pan tightly. Cook chicken slowly 25 to 40 minutes, or until all pieces are tender. For crisp skin, uncover chicken the last 10 minutes of cooking.

3 or 4 servings

Chicken Cacciatore

Cacciatore, meaning "hunter" in Italian, indicates that the food (usually chicken), is prepared in the "hunter's style," that is, simmering the fowl in a well-seasoned tomato and wine sauce.

¼ cup cooking oil
1 broiler-fryer (2½ pounds), cut up
2 onions, sliced
2 cloves garlic, minced
3 tomatoes, cored and quartered
2 green peppers, sliced
1 small bay leaf
1 teaspoon salt
¼ teaspoon pepper
½ teaspoon celery seed
1 teaspoon crushed oregano or
    basil
1 can (8 ounces) tomato sauce
¼ cup sauterne
8 ounces spaghetti, cooked
    according to package directions

1. Heat oil in a large, heavy skillet; add chicken and brown on all sides. Remove from skillet.
2. Add onion and garlic to oil remaining in skillet and cook until onion is tender, but not brown; stir occasionally.
3. Return chicken to skillet and add the tomatoes, green pepper, and bay leaf.
4. Mix salt, pepper, celery seed, and oregano and blend with tomato sauce; pour over all.
5. Cover and cook over low heat 45 minutes. Blend in wine and cook, uncovered, 20 minutes longer. Discard bay leaf.
6. Put the cooked spaghetti onto a hot serving platter and top with the chicken and sauce.

About 6 servings

Liver and Onions, Italian Style
(Fegato con Cipolla)

1½ pounds beef liver, sliced about
    ¼ to ½ inch thick
½ cup flour
1 teaspoon salt
⅛ teaspoon pepper
2 onions, thinly sliced
⅓ cup olive oil
½ cup Marsala

1. If necessary, remove tubes and membrane from liver; cut liver into serving-size pieces.
2. Coat liver with a mixture of flour, salt, and pepper; set aside.
3. Cook onions until tender in hot oil in a large skillet. Remove onions and add liver. Brown on both sides over medium heat.
4. Return onions to skillet; add the wine. Bring to boiling and cook 1 minute. Serve at once.

4 or 5 servings

Liver and Onions with Mushrooms: Follow recipe for Liver and Onions, Italian Style. Add **1 cup drained canned whole mushrooms** with the Marsala.

Fried Scampi (Scampi Fritti)

3 pounds fresh prawns or shrimp
    with shells
    Fat for deep frying heated to
    360°F
½ cup olive oil
4 cloves garlic, minced
1 teaspoon salt
½ teaspoon oregano
¼ teaspoon pepper
1 teaspoon chopped parsley

1. Wash prawns in cold water. Remove tiny legs, peel off shells, and devein prawns. Rinse in cold water, then pat dry with absorbent paper.
2. Put only as many prawns in fat as will float uncrowded one layer deep. Fry 3 to 5 minutes, or until golden brown. Drain over fat before removing to absorbent paper. Turn fried prawns onto a warm platter.
3. Heat oil in a skillet. Add garlic, salt, oregano, and pepper and cook until garlic is lightly browned. Pour sauce over prawns and sprinkle with parsley.

About 6 servings

Lobster Fra Diavolo (Aragosta alla Diavola)

    Marinara Sauce (page 82)
2 live lobsters (about 1½ pounds
    each)
½ cup red wine
    Few grains cayenne pepper

1. Prepare Marinara Sauce.
2. While sauce is cooking, fill a large, deep kettle about two thirds full with water. Bring to boiling and plunge lobsters, one at a time, head first into boiling water. Cover and boil about 8 minutes (Lobsters will turn pink.) Remove lobsters with tongs. With a sharp knife, slit underside lengthwise and remove stomach, lungs, and vein. Keep warm.
3. When sauce is cooked, stir in wine and cayenne, bring to boiling, and pour over lobsters. Serve immediately.

2 servings

Scampi Flamingo

A recipe from the Danieli Royal Excelsior in Venice.

½ cup butter
1 cup chopped celery
¼ cup chopped carrot
¼ cup chopped onion
¼ teaspoon thyme
2 pounds fresh shrimp with shells
3 tablespoons cognac
2 cups light cream
⅓ cup sherry
½ cup butter
½ teaspoon lemon juice
⅛ teaspoon ground nutmeg
¼ cup Béchamel Sauce (page 83)

1. Heat ½ cup butter in a large skillet. Sauté vegetables with thyme until lightly browned. Add the shrimp and brown carefully.
2. Add cognac and flame it. Add cream, sherry, and sauce; cook 15 minutes.
3. Remove shrimp; shell and devein them; keep warm.
4. Add ½ cup butter, lemon juice, and nutmeg to sauce; cook about 5 minutes. Strain through a fine sieve and pour over the shrimp.
5. Serve sauce and shrimp with hot cooked rice.

About 4 servings

Fillet of Sole in White Wine
(Filetti di Sogliole al Vino)

2 pounds sole fillets
½ cup dry white wine
½ cup chopped onion
3 tablespoons butter, melted
2 bay leaves, crushed
1 teaspoon chopped parsley
½ teaspoon salt
¼ teaspoon pepper

1. Put fillets into a greased shallow 2-quart casserole.
2. Mix wine, onion, butter, and dry seasonings. Pour over fish. Cover casserole.
3. Bake at 375°F 25 minutes, or until fish flakes easily when tested with a fork.

6 servings

Cod Sailor Style (Baccalà alla Marinara)

2 pounds cod steaks, about 1 inch thick
2 cups canned tomatoes, sieved
¼ cup chopped green olives
2 tablespoons capers
1 tablespoon parsley
1 teaspoon salt
½ teaspoon pepper
½ teaspoon oregano

1. Put cod steaks into a greased 1½-quart casserole.
2. Combine tomatoes, olives, capers, parsley, salt, pepper, and oregano in a saucepan. Bring to boiling and pour over cod.
3. Bake at 350°F 25 to 30 minutes, or until fish flakes easily when tested with a fork.

4 servings

VEGETABLES

Asparagus Parmesan (Asparagi alla Parmigiana)

1½ pounds asparagus
½ cup butter, melted
½ cup grated Parmesan or Romano cheese
1 teaspoon salt
½ teaspoon pepper

1. Wash asparagus. Put into a small amount of boiling salted water in a skillet. Bring to boiling, reduce heat, and cook 5 minutes, uncovered; cover and cook 10 minutes, or until just tender.
2. Pour melted butter into a greased 1½-quart casserole. Put cooked asparagus into casserole and sprinkle with mixture of grated cheese, salt, and pepper.
3. Bake at 450°F 5 to 10 minutes, or until cheese is melted.

About 6 servings

Green Beans with Onions (Fagiolini con Cipolla)

8 to 12 small whole onions, peeled
1 pound green beans
¼ teaspoon salt
2 tablespoons olive oil
1 clove garlic, chopped
½ teaspoon salt
⅛ teaspoon pepper

1. Put onions into a small amount of boiling salted water in a saucepan. Cover and cook 15 to 20 minutes, or until onions are tender.
2. Meanwhile, wash beans, break off ends, and cut beans lengthwise into fine strips. Bring a small amount of water to boiling in a saucepan, add ¼ teaspoon salt and beans. Cover and cook 10 to 15 minutes, or until beans are tender. Drain.
3. Heat oil and garlic in a skillet until garlic is lightly browned. Add green beans and onions, season with salt and pepper, and cook 5 to 10 minutes, or until thoroughly heated, stirring occasionally.

About 4 servings

Green Beans in Sauce (Fagiolini al Sugo)

2 tablespoons olive oil
1 clove garlic, chopped
2½ cups canned tomatoes, sieved
1 cup boiling water
½ teaspoon salt
⅛ teaspoon pepper
⅛ teaspoon oregano
2 teaspoons chopped parsley
1 pound green beans
¼ teaspoon salt

1. Heat olive oil and garlic in a skillet until garlic is lightly browned. Add tomatoes and water slowly. Stir in ½ teaspoon salt, pepper, oregano, and parsley. Bring to boiling, cover, and simmer 20 minutes, stirring occasionally.
2. Meanwhile, wash beans, break off ends, and cut crosswise into pieces. Bring a small amount of water to boiling in a saucepan. Add ¼ teaspoon salt and beans. Cover and cook about 15 minutes, or until beans are tender. Drain.
3. Turn beans into a warm serving bowl and pour sauce over them. Serve immediately.

About 4 servings

Broccoli, Southern Style

1 medium onion, thinly sliced
1 clove garlic, thinly sliced
2 tablespoons olive oil
1½ tablespoons flour
½ teaspoon salt
⅛ teaspoon pepper
1 cup chicken broth
4 anchovy fillets, chopped
½ cup sliced ripe olives
2 cups shredded process Cheddar
  cheese
2 pounds broccoli, cooked and
  drained

1. Cook onion and garlic in hot olive oil in a saucepan until onion is soft. Blend in a mixture of flour, salt, and pepper. Heat until bubbly.
2. Add chicken broth, stirring constantly. Bring to boiling and cook 1 or 2 minutes, or until sauce thickens.
3. Blend in anchovies, olives, and cheese. Pour sauce over hot broccoli.

About 6 servings

Italian Cauliflower (Cavolfiore Italiana)

1 large head cauliflower, washed
  and trimmed
2 tablespoons butter
½ clove garlic, minced
2 teaspoons flour
1 teaspoon salt
2 cups canned tomatoes
1 small green pepper, coarsely
  chopped
¼ teaspoon oregano

1. Separate cauliflower into flowerets. Put into a saucepan containing a small amount of boiling salted water. Cook, uncovered, 5 minutes. Cover and cook 8 to 10 minutes, or until cauliflower is tender. Drain if necessary and keep hot.
2. Heat butter with garlic; stir in flour and salt and cook until bubbly.
3. Add tomatoes and bring to boiling, stirring constantly; cook 1 to 2 minutes. Mix in green pepper and oregano.
4. Pour sauce over hot cauliflower.

About 6 servings

Baked Eggplant (Melanzane alla Sardegna)

4 eggplants (about ¾ pound each)
½ cup olive oil
2 teaspoons salt
1 teaspoon pepper

1. Wash and dry eggplants; remove stems. Leave eggplant whole and unpeeled. Make a slit the length of each eggplant only to the center, not completely through to the other side.
2. In each slit, drizzle 1 tablespoon olive oil and season with ½ teaspoon salt and ¼ teaspoon pepper. Gently press eggplant together and rub completely with olive oil. Rub an 11×7-inch baking dish with olive oil. Place eggplants in dish.
3. Bake at 375°F about 30 minutes, or until eggplants are tender.

6 to 8 servings

Eggplant Parmesan (Melanzane alla Parmigiana)

Tomato Meat Sauce (page 84)
4 quarts water
1 tablespoon salt
3 cups (about 8 ounces) noodles
1 eggplant (about 1 pound)
2 eggs, slightly beaten
¼ cup cream
3 tablespoons olive oil
⅔ cup fine dry bread crumbs
1 cup grated Parmesan cheese
6 slices (3 ounces) mozzarella
cheese

1. Prepare Tomato Meat Sauce.
2. Heat water in a large saucepan. Add salt, then noodles; stir with a fork. Boil rapidly. uncovered, 10 to 15 minutes, or until noodles are tender. Drain. Set aside.
3. Wash eggplant, pare, and cut into ½-inch-thick slices.
4. Combine eggs and cream.
5. Heat oil in a skillet. Dip eggplant into egg mixture, then into bread crumbs. Put eggplant slices into skillet and brown slowly on both sides.
6. Put a third of the drained noodles into a greased 2-quart casserole. Layer with a third of eggplant slices. Add 1 cup meat sauce. Sprinkle with a third of grated cheese. Repeat layers, ending with eggplant slices. Top with cheese slices. Cover casserole.
7. Bake at 350°F about 20 minutes. Remove cover and bake 10 to 15 minutes, or until cheese is lightly browned. Serve with remaining meat sauce.

About 6 servings

Mushrooms Parmesan (Funghi alla Parmigiana)

1 pound mushrooms with 1- to
2-inch caps
2 tablespoons olive oil
¼ cup chopped onion
½ clove garlic, finely chopped
⅓ cup fine dry bread crumbs
3 tablespoons grated Parmesan
cheese
1 tablespoon chopped parsley
½ teaspoon salt
⅛ teaspoon oregano
2 tablespoons olive oil

1. Clean mushrooms and remove stems. Place caps open-end up in a shallow greased 1½-quart baking dish; set aside. Finely chop mushroom stems.
2. Heat 2 tablespoons olive oil in a skillet. Add mushroom stems, onion, and garlic. Cook slowly until onion and garlic are slightly browned.
3. Combine bread crumbs, cheese, parsley, salt, and oregano. Mix in the onion, garlic, and mushroom stems. Lightly fill mushroom caps with mixture. Pour 2 tablespoons olive oil into the baking dish.
4. Bake at 400°F 15 to 20 minutes, or until mushrooms are tender and tops are browned.

6 to 8 servings

Anchovy-Stuffed Mushrooms: Follow recipe for Mushrooms Parmesan. Omit cheese. Mix in **4 anchovy fillets,** finely chopped.

Stuffed Onions *(Cipolle Imbottite)*

6 large onions
2 tablespoons butter
1 cup soft bread crumbs
2 tablespoons olive oil
¼ pound ground beef
2 cups soft bread crumbs
1 egg yolk
2 teaspoons chopped parsley
1 teaspoon salt
¼ teaspoon pepper
¼ teaspoon marjoram
2 tablespoons olive oil
1 tablespoon chopped parsley

1. Cut off root ends of onions; peel, rinse, and cut off a ½-inch slice from top of each.
2. Put onions in boiling salted water to cover in a large saucepan. Cook 10 to 15 minutes, or until onions are slightly tender. Drain well and cool.
3. Meanwhile, heat butter in a skillet. Stir in 1 cup bread crumbs. Turn into a small bowl and set aside.
4. With a sharp knife, cut down around onions, about ¼ inch from edge, leaving about 3 outside layers. With a spoon, scoop out centers and chop them.
5. Heat 2 tablespoons oil in skillet. Add chopped onion and ground beef to heated oil; cook until beef is browned.
6. Combine beef mixture with 2 cups bread crumbs, egg yolk, 2 teaspoons parsley, salt, pepper, and marjoram. Lightly fill onions with mixture.
7. Put filled onions into a greased 2½-quart casserole. Spoon buttered crumbs on top and sprinkle with remaining oil and parsley.
8. Bake at 350°F about 1 hour.

6 servings

Stuffed Peppers *(Peperoni Imbottiti)*

4 green peppers
¼ cup olive oil
1 pound ground beef
1⅓ cups cooked rice
2 tablespoons minced onion
1 tablespoon minced parsley
½ teaspoon salt
¼ teaspoon pepper
1½ cups canned tomatoes, sieved
¼ cup water
¼ cup minced celery
1 tablespoon olive oil
½ teaspoon salt
¼ teaspoon pepper
Mozzarella cheese, cut in strips

1. Rinse peppers and cut a thin slice from stem end of each. Remove white fiber and seeds; rinse. Drop peppers into boiling salted water to cover and simmer 5 minutes. Remove peppers from water; invert and set aside to drain.
2. Heat ¼ cup oil in a skillet. Add ground beef and cook until browned. Stir in cooked rice, onion, parsley, ½ teaspoon salt, and ¼ teaspoon pepper. Lightly fill peppers with rice-meat mixture, heaping slightly. Set in a 2-quart baking dish.
3. Mix tomatoes, water, celery, and remaining oil, salt, and pepper; pour around peppers. Put strips of cheese on each pepper.
4. Bake at 350°F about 15 minutes.

4 servings

Baked Tomatoes, Genoa Style
(Pomodori alla Genovese)

4 firm ripe tomatoes, cut in halves and seeded
Sugar
¼ cup olive oil
2 cloves garlic, minced
1½ teaspoons salt
½ teaspoon pepper
1½ teaspoons marjoram, crushed
¼ cup finely snipped parsley
½ cup shredded Parmesan cheese

1. Put tomato halves, cut side up, in a shallow baking dish. Sprinkle lightly with sugar.
2. Mix olive oil, garlic, salt, pepper, and marjoram. Spoon an equal amount onto each tomato half. Sprinkle with parsley and cheese.
3. Bake at 350°F about 20 minutes, or until lightly browned.

4 servings

Deep-Fried Potatoes

Fat for deep frying heated to 360°F
2 pounds potatoes (about 6 medium)
Salt

1. Start heating fat for deep frying.
2. Wash and pare potatoes. Trim off sides and ends to form large blocks. Cut lengthwise into sticks about ⅜ inch wide. Pat dry with absorbent paper.
3. Fry about 1 cup of potatoes at a time in hot fat until potatoes are tender and golden brown. Drain over fat, then put on paper toweling. Sprinkle with salt.
4. Serve hot.

About 4 servings

Zucchini Parmesan (Zucchini alla Parmigiana)

8 to 10 small zucchini squash (about 2½ pounds)
3 tablespoons olive oil
⅔ cup coarsely chopped onion
¼ pound mushrooms, cleaned and sliced
⅔ cup grated Parmesan cheese
2 cans (6 ounces each) tomato paste
1 clove garlic, minced
1 teaspoon salt
⅛ teaspoon pepper

1. Wash and trim off ends of zucchini; cut crosswise into ⅛-inch-thick slices.
2. Heat olive oil in a large saucepan; add zucchini, onion, and mushrooms. Cover saucepan and cook vegetables over low heat 10 to 15 minutes, or until tender, stirring occasionally.
3. Remove vegetable mixture from heat; stir in about half the cheese. Combine tomato paste, garlic, salt, and pepper; pour into vegetable mixture, blending lightly but thoroughly. Turn mixture into a 2-quart casserole. Sprinkle with remaining cheese.
4. Bake at 350°F 20 to 30 minutes.

About 8 servings

Zucchini in Salsa Verde

Fat for deep frying
¼ cup olive oil
2 tablespoons wine vinegar
2 tablespoons minced parsley
1 clove garlic, crushed in a garlic press or minced
2 anchovy fillets, finely chopped
Few grains black pepper
4 zucchini squash, washed and thinly sliced
Flour
Salt

1. Start heating the fat to 365°F.
2. Meanwhile, blend oil, vinegar, parsley, garlic, anchovies, and pepper in a small bowl and set mixture aside.
3. Coat zucchini slices slightly with flour. Fry in hot fat, turning frequently, until lightly browned (2 to 3 minutes). Remove from fat and drain. Sprinkle lightly with salt.
4. Put zucchini into a bowl; pour the sauce over it and toss lightly to coat well. Cover and set aside at least an hour before serving.

4 servings

Zucchini Romano

8 small zucchini (about 1½ pounds)
1 egg, fork beaten
½ cup shredded mozzarella cheese
3 tablespoons bottled Italian salad dressing
¹⁄₁₆ teaspoon black pepper
2 tablespoons melted butter or margarine
½ pound ground ham or veal
½ cup Quick Italian Tomato Sauce (page 83)

1. Wash zucchini and trim ends. Slice off a narrow lengthwise strip. Using an apple corer, remove seeds to make a hollow about ¾ inch deep in each zucchini. Cover with boiling water, simmer about 5 minutes, and drain well.
2. Meanwhile, combine egg, cheese, dressing, pepper, and butter in a bowl. (If using veal, add ¼ teaspoon salt.) Lightly mix in meat. Fill zucchini with meat mixture, using about 3 tablespoons in each hollow.
3. Arrange zucchini, stuffed side up, in a single layer in an oiled shallow 1½-quart baking dish; spread tops with sauce. (Or omit sauce and brush tops with olive oil.)
4. Bake at 375°F about 15 minutes, or until meat is cooked. Serve hot.

8 servings

 SALADS

Red Kidney Bean Salad (Insalata di Fagioli)

1 can (16 ounces) kidney beans
¼ cup wine vinegar
3 tablespoons olive oil
¼ teaspoon oregano
¼ teaspoon salt
⅛ teaspoon pepper
¼ cup sliced celery
2 tablespoons chopped onion
Lettuce cups

1. Thoroughly rinse and drain kidney beans.
2. Combine vinegar, oil, oregano, salt, and pepper; mix with beans. Blend in celery and onion; chill.
3. Serve in crisp lettuce cups.

About 4 servings

Italian Potato Salad (Insalata di Patate)

2 medium potatoes, boiled, peeled, and diced
⅓ cup chopped celery
½ cup diced pared cucumber
½ cup chopped ripe olives
2 tablespoons minced onion
¾ cup Italian Dressing (below)
¼ teaspoon oregano

1. Lightly toss together the potatoes, celery, cucumber, olives, and onion. With a fork, thoroughly but carefully blend in the dressing mixed with oregano.
2. Cover the salad. Chill about 1 hour before serving.

About 4 servings

Green Salad (Insalata Verde)

1 large head lettuce, or an equal amount of another salad green (curly endive, romaine, escarole, chicory, or dandelion greens)
1 clove garlic
Italian Dressing

1. Wash lettuce in cold water, removing core, separating leaves, and removing any bruised leaves. Drain; dry thoroughly and carefully. Tear lettuce into bite-size pieces, put into a plastic bag, and chill 1 hour.
2. Just before serving, cut garlic in half and rub a wooden bowl. Put greens in bowl and pour on desired amount of dressing. Turn and toss the greens until well coated with dressing and no dressing remains in the bottom of the bowl.

About 6 servings

Green Salad with Anchovy Dressing:
Follow recipe for Green Salad. Add **2 tomatoes,** cut in wedges, **¼ cup diced celery,** and **½ cup chopped ripe olives** to lettuce in bowl. Toss with **Anchovy Dressing.**

Mixed Salad:
Follow recipe for Green Salad. Add **¼ cup chopped cucumber, ¼ cup chopped celery, ¼ cup sliced radishes,** and **¼ cup chopped ripe olives** to lettuce before tossing with dressing.

Italian Dressing

6 tablespoons olive oil
3 tablespoons wine vinegar
1 clove garlic, crushed in a garlic press
¼ teaspoon salt
⅛ teaspoon pepper

1. Place all ingredients in a screw-top jar, shake well, and chill.
2. Just before serving, beat or shake thoroughly.

About ½ cup dressing

Anchovy Dressing:
Follow recipe for Italian Dressing. Add **1 teaspoon prepared mustard** and **2 finely chopped anchovy fillets** to jar before shaking.

Chicken Vesuvio, 42, from Campania

Broccoli Salad *(Insalata di Broccoli)*

1 pound broccoli
3 tablespoons olive oil
3 tablespoons lemon juice
1 medium clove garlic
¼ teaspoon salt
⅛ teaspoon pepper

1. Trim off leaves and bottoms of broccoli stalks, and split thick stems lengthwise. Cook, covered, in a small amount of salted water until just tender. Drain and chill.
2. Combine olive oil, lemon juice, garlic, salt, and pepper. Drizzle over thoroughly chilled broccoli and serve.

About 3 servings

Cauliflower Salad: Follow recipe for Broccoli Salad. Substitute **1 medium head cauliflower** for broccoli. Separate into flowerets and cook as for broccoli. Peel and dice **1 boiled potato**; combine with cauliflower and chill. Substitute **wine vinegar** for the lemon juice and add ¼ **teaspoon oregano.**

Green Bean Salad: Follow recipe for Broccoli Salad. Clean and cook ½ **pound green beans** and substitute for broccoli. Use wine vinegar instead of lemon juice.

Asparagus Salad: Follow recipe for Broccoli Salad. Clean and cook **1 pound asparagus** and substitute for the broccoli.

Pickled Pepper Salad *(Insalata di Peperoni)*

2 cups sliced pickled red peppers
¾ cup chopped celery
½ cup sliced ripe olives
8 anchovy fillets, chopped
2 tablespoons olive oil
2 tablespoons wine vinegar
¼ teaspoon oregano
⅛ teaspoon salt
¼ teaspoon pepper

1. Gently combine the red peppers, celery, olives, and anchovy fillets. Mix oil, vinegar, oregano, salt, and pepper; pour over the red pepper mixture. Toss gently.
2. Serve very cold.

6 to 8 servings

SAUCES

Butter and Garlic Sauce *(Salsa al Burro e Aglio)*

¾ cup butter
2 cloves garlic, peeled and thinly sliced
¼ cup water
½ teaspoon finely chopped parsley

1. Melt butter in skillet. Stir in garlic and cook slowly until slightly browned. Remove from heat and cool slightly.
2. Slowly add water and parsley. Cook about 10 minutes and serve over **cooked spaghetti.**

About 1 cup sauce

Butter and Cheese Sauce: Follow recipe for Butter and Garlic Sauce. Omit garlic. Mix butter sauce with spaghetti and sprinkle with ¼ **cup grated Parmesan cheese.**

Eggplant Pugliese Style, 44, from Apulia

Clam Sauce (Salsa di Vongole)

¼ cup finely chopped onion
3 tablespoons butter
2 tablespoons flour
¼ teaspoon salt
⅛ teaspoon white pepper
1 can (12 ounces) clam juice
3 tablespoons finely chopped
    parsley
¼ to ½ teaspoon thyme
1 jar (7½ ounces) whole clams,
    drained and cut in pieces
1 can (2½ ounces) minced clams,
    drained

1. Add onion to hot butter in a saucepan and cook until soft. Blend in a mixture of flour, salt, and pepper. Heat until bubbly.
2. Remove from heat and add the clam juice gradually, stirring constantly. Mix in parsley and thyme. Bring to boiling; stir and cook 1 to 2 minutes. Stir in the clams; heat thoroughly.

About 2¼ cups sauce

Tomato Sauce with Meat

1 cup chopped onion
1 clove garlic, minced
3 tablespoons olive oil
½ pound ground beef
½ pound ground pork
1 can (28 ounces) Italian-style
    tomatoes, drained
3 cans (6 ounces each) tomato
    paste
2 cups water
2½ teaspoons salt
½ teaspoon pepper
1 teaspoon oregano

1. Add the onion and garlic to hot oil in a large, deep skillet and cook until onion is soft.
2. Add the ground meat, separate it into small pieces, and cook until lightly browned. Stir in tomatoes, tomato paste, water, and a mixture of salt, pepper, and oregano. Cook, uncovered, over low heat about 1 hour, stirring occasionally.

About 7½ cups sauce

Marinara Sauce

2 medium cloves garlic, sliced
½ cup olive oil
1 can (28 ounces) tomatoes,
    sieved
1¼ teaspoons salt
⅛ teaspoon pepper
1 teaspoon oregano
¼ teaspoon chopped parsley

1. Brown garlic in hot olive oil in a large, deep skillet. Add gradually, stirring constantly, a mixture of the tomatoes, salt, pepper, oregano, and parsley. Cook rapidly uncovered about 15 minutes, or until sauce is thickened; stir occasionally. If sauce becomes too thick, stir in ¼ to ½ cup water.
2. Serve sauce hot on **cooked spaghetti.**

4 cups sauce

Medium White Sauce

2 tablespoons butter
2 tablespoons flour
½ teaspoon salt
⅛ teaspoon pepper
1 cup milk (use light cream for a richer sauce)

1. Heat butter in a saucepan. Blend in flour, salt, and pepper; heat and stir until bubbly.
2. Gradually add the milk, stirring until smooth. Bring to boiling; cook and stir 1 to 2 minutes longer.

About 1 cup

Thick White Sauce: Follow recipe for Medium White Sauce. Use 3 to 4 tablespoons flour and 3 to 4 tablespoons butter.

Thin White Sauce: Follow recipe for Medium White Sauce. Use 1 tablespoon flour and 1 tablespoon butter.

Béchamel Sauce: Follow recipe for Medium White Sauce. Substitute ½ **cup chicken broth** for ½ cup milk; use ½ cup cream for remaining liquid needed. Stir in **1 tablespoon minced onion.**

Quick Italian Tomato Sauce (Salsa di Pomodoro)

1 cup chopped onion
¼ cup olive oil or cooking oil
1 clove garlic, minced
¼ cup grated carrot
1 tablespoon finely snipped parsley
¼ teaspoon basil, crushed
⅛ teaspoon thyme, crushed
2 cans (8 ounces each) tomato sauce
½ cup beef broth (dissolve ½ beef bouillon cube in ½ cup boiling water)

1. Add onion to hot oil in a saucepan and cook until tender. Stir in the garlic, carrot, and parsley; cook about 3 minutes, stirring frequently.
2. Blend in remaining ingredients. Simmer gently until flavors are blended (about 10 minutes).

About 3 cups sauce

Green Sauce (Salsa Verde)

1 tablespoon chopped parsley
1 tablespoon chopped watercress
1 tablespoon chopped capers
1 small clove garlic, peeled and chopped
¼ teaspoon salt
⅛ teaspoon pepper
6 tablespoons olive oil
3 tablespoons lemon juice

1. Place parsley, watercress, capers, garlic, salt, and pepper in a mortar. Crush with a pestle to make a smooth paste.
2. Add olive oil, 1 tablespoon at a time, beating vigorously with a fork or spoon after each addition. Slowly add lemon juice, beating constantly.
3. Serve with **artichokes, cooked spaghetti, shrimp,** or **any fried fish.**

About ½ cup sauce

Tomato Meat Sauce (Ragù di Pomodoro)

¼ cup olive oil
½ cup chopped onion
½ pound beef chuck
½ pound pork shoulder
7 cups canned tomatoes with liquid, sieved
1 tablespoon salt
1 bay leaf
1 can (6 ounces) tomato paste

1. Heat olive oil in a large saucepot. Add onion and cook until lightly browned. Add the meat and brown on all sides. Stir in tomatoes and salt. Add bay leaf. Cover and simmer about 2½ hours.

2. Stir tomato paste into sauce. Simmer, uncovered, stirring occasionally, about 2 hours, or until thickened. If sauce becomes too thick, add ½ **cup water.**

3. Remove meat and bay leaf from sauce (use meat as desired). Serve sauce over **cooked spaghetti.**

About 4 cups sauce

Tomato Sauce with Ground Meat: Follow recipe for Tomato Meat Sauce. Brown ½ **pound ground beef** in **3 tablespoons olive oil,** breaking beef into small pieces. After removing meat from sauce, add ground beef and simmer 10 minutes longer.

Tomato Sauce with Mushrooms: Follow recipe for Tomato Meat Sauce. Clean and slice ½ **pound mushrooms.** Cook slowly in 3 tablespoons melted butter until lightly browned. After removing meat from sauce, add mushrooms and simmer 10 minutes longer.

Tomato Sauce with Chicken Livers: Follow recipe for Tomato Meat Sauce. Rinse and pat dry ½ **pound chicken livers.** Slice livers and brown in **3 tablespoons olive oil.** After removing meat from sauce, add livers and simmer 10 minutes longer.

Tomato Sauce with Sausage: Follow recipe for Tomato Meat Sauce. Brown about ½ **pound Italian sausage,** cut in 2-inch pieces, in **1 tablespoon olive oil.** After removing meat from sauce, add sausage and simmer 10 minutes longer.

Oil and Garlic Sauce (Salsa all' Olio e Aglio)

½ cup olive oil
4 cloves garlic, thinly sliced
½ cup water
1 tablespoon chopped parsley
⅛ teaspoon pepper

1. Heat olive oil in a skillet. Stir in garlic and cook until browned. Remove skillet from heat and cool slightly.

2. Slowly stir in water. Add parsley and pepper. Simmer about 10 minutes. Serve over **cooked spaghetti.**

About 1 cup sauce

Garlic Sauce with Anchovies: Follow recipe for Oil and Garlic Sauce. Stir in **5 chopped anchovy fillets** with the parsley.

Garlic Sauce with Walnuts: Follow recipe for Oil and Garlic Sauce. Add **2 tablespoons chopped walnuts** with the parsley.

Garlic Sauce with Capers: Follow recipe for Oil and Garlic Sauce. Add **2 tablespoons capers** with the parsley.

Oil and Onion Sauce: Follow recipe for Oil and Garlic Sauce, substituting **1 medium onion,** thinly sliced, for the garlic.

Bolognese Meat Sauce (Ragù Bolognese)

2 tablespoons butter
1 medium onion, finely chopped
1 small carrot, finely chopped
1 small stalk celery, finely chopped
¾ pound ground beef
¼ pound ground lean pork
¼ cup tomato sauce or tomato paste
½ cup white wine
1 cup beef broth or stock
½ teaspoon salt
¼ teaspoon pepper

1. Melt butter in a skillet. Stir in onion, carrot, and celery. Cook until tender. Add meat and cook over low heat 10 to 15 minutes.
2. Add tomato sauce, wine, ¼ cup broth, salt, and pepper; mix well. Simmer about 1¼ hours. Stir in remaining broth, a small amount at a time, while the sauce is simmering. Sauce should be thick.

About 2½ cups sauce

Italian Strawberry Water Ice (Granita di Fragole)

2 cups sugar
1 cup water
4 pints fresh ripe strawberries, rinsed and hulled
⅓ cup orange juice
¼ cup lemon juice

1. Combine sugar and water in a saucepan; stir and bring to boiling. Boil 5 minutes; let cool.
2. Purée the strawberries in an electric blender or force through a sieve or food mill. Add juices to a mixture of the cooked syrup and strawberries; mix well.
3. Turn into refrigerator trays, cover tightly, and freeze.
4. About 45 minutes before serving time, remove trays from freezer to refrigerator to allow the ice to soften slightly. Spoon into sherbet glasses or other serving dishes.

About 2 quarts water ice

Biscuit Tortoni

⅓ cup confectioners' sugar
1 tablespoon sherry
½ cup plus 2 tablespoons fine dry
    macaroon crumbs
1 cup whipping cream, whipped
1 egg white

1. Fold sugar, sherry, and ½ cup macaroon crumbs into whipped cream until well blended.
2. Beat egg white until stiff, not dry, peaks are formed. Fold into whipped cream mixture.
3. Divide mixture equally into ten 2-inch heavy paper baking cups and sprinkle with the remaining crumbs. Freeze until firm.

10 servings

Italian Fried Twists (Cenci)

¼ cup butter
4 cups cake flour
⅓ cup sugar
4 eggs
2 tablespoons brandy
    Oil or shortening for deep frying
    Confectioners' sugar

1. In a large bowl, cut butter into flour with a pastry blender until the mixture resembles coarse crumbs. Stir in sugar.
2. In a small bowl, lightly beat the eggs with brandy. Add to flour mixture, stirring until all the flour is moistened. On a lightly floured surface, knead dough until smooth (about 5 minutes). Cover and let rest 10 minutes.
3. Fill a heavy saucepan with oil 4 inches deep; slowly heat to 400°F. Cut off a sixth of the dough at a time, and roll paper thin. Using a pastry cutter or sharp knife, cut into 8 × ¾-inch strips. Leave in strips or tie in knots. If desired, dough may also be cut in 2-inch-long diamonds.
4. Gently drop into hot oil, a few at a time, and cook 1 minute, or until lightly browned. Using a slotted spoon or tongs, lift out of oil and drain on paper towels. Cool slightly.
5. Sprinkle generously with confectioners' sugar and store, loosely covered, in a dry place.

About 8 dozen twists

Italian Butter Cookies (Canestrelli)

4 cups sifted all-purpose flour
1 cup sugar
2½ teaspoons grated lemon peel
1 tablespoon rum
4 egg yolks, beaten
1 cup firm unsalted butter, cut in
    pieces
1 egg white, slightly beaten

1. Combine flour, sugar, and lemon peel in a large bowl; mix thoroughly. Add rum and then egg yolks in fourths, mixing thoroughly after each addition.
2. Cut butter into flour mixture with pastry blender until particles are fine. Work with fingertips until a dough is formed.
3. Roll one half of dough at a time about ¼ inch thick on a lightly floured surface. Cut into desired shapes. Brush tops with egg white. Transfer to lightly greased cookie sheets.
4. Bake at 350°F about 15 minutes.

About 6 dozen cookies

Zuppa Inglese

Zuppa Inglese, which means English soup, probably has more variations and stories about its origin than any other Italian food. That a rum-soaked cake should be called English soup has given much cause for comment on the origin of this wrongly named delicacy. Perhaps the most logical explanation has been that the name was given to tease the English about their love of rum, and the first Zuppa was so rum-soaked that it had to be eaten with a soup spoon.

Italian Sponge Cake
½ **cup rum**
2 **tablespoons cold water**
Pineapple Cream Filling (page 88), chilled
Chocolate Cream Filling (page 88), chilled
Whipped Cream (page 89)
Candied cherries

1. Trim corners of each of the sponge cake layers to form ovals. Save all pieces trimmed from cake. Place one layer on a platter; set other two aside.
2. Combine rum and water. Sprinkle a third of rum mixture over first cake layer and spread with desired amount of Pineapple Cream Filling. Top with second layer, sprinkle with half the remaining rum mixture, and spread with desired amount of Chocolate Cream Filling.
3. Place third layer on cake and sprinkle with remaining rum mixture. Cover cake with waxed paper and chill several hours.
4. Make a square, diamond, or heart shape from leftover pieces of cake. Place on top of cake and frost cake with Whipped Cream. If desired, decorate with Whipped Cream using a No. 27 star decorating tip. Garnish with candied cherries.
5. Store dessert in refrigerator until ready to serve.

16 to 20 servings

Note: If desired, **Seven-Minute Frosting (page 88)** or **Butter Frosting (page 88)** may be used to frost and decorate the dessert.

Italian Sponge Cake *(Pan di Spagna)*

5 **egg yolks**
½ **cup sugar**
2 **tablespoons lemon juice**
1 **teaspoon grated lemon peel**
1 **teaspoon vanilla extract**
½ **teaspoon salt**
5 **egg whites**
½ **cup sugar**
1 **cup sifted cake flour**

1. Combine egg yolks, ½ cup sugar, lemon juice, lemon peel, and vanilla extract. Beat 3 to 4 minutes with an electric mixer on medium-high speed; set aside.
2. Add salt to egg whites and beat until frothy. Gradually add ½ cup sugar, beating constantly until stiff peaks are formed.
3. Gently fold egg yolk mixture into beaten egg whites. Sift flour over the egg mixture, ¼ cup at a time, gently folding until just blended after each addition. Turn batter into a 9-inch tube pan (see Note).
4. Bake at 325°F 60 to 65 minutes, or until cake springs back when lightly touched or when a cake tester or wooden pick inserted comes out clean.
5. Invert and leave cake in pan until completely cooled.

One 9-inch tube cake

Note: For Zuppa Inglese, pour batter into three 11×7×1½-inch baking pans. Bake at 325°F 30 to 35 minutes.

Pineapple Cream Filling (*Crema d'Ananasso*)

½ cup sugar
2 tablespoons cornstarch
⅛ teaspoon salt
½ cup cold milk
1½ cups milk, scalded
3 eggs, slightly beaten
1 can (20 ounces) crushed
　　pineapple, drained
1 teaspoon vanilla extract

1. Combine sugar, cornstarch, and salt in a saucepan. Gradually add cold milk, stirring well. Slowly stir in the scalded milk.
2. Stirring gently and constantly, rapidly bring mixture to boiling over direct heat and cook 3 minutes. Pour into top of double boiler and place over simmering water. Cover and cook about 12 minutes, stirring three or four times.
3. Vigorously stir about 3 tablespoons hot mixture into the eggs. Immediately blend into mixture in double boiler. Cook over simmering water 3 to 5 minutes. Stir slowly so mixture cooks evenly. Remove from heat and cool.
4. Stir in pineapple and vanilla extract. Chill.

About 4 cups filling

Chocolate Cream Filling: Follow recipe for Pineapple Cream Filling. Add **1½ ounces (1½ squares) unsweetened chocolate** to milk before scalding. Beat smooth with a rotary beater. Increase sugar to ⅔ cup and omit the pineapple.

About 2½ cups filling

Butter Frosting (*Ghiacciata di Burro*)

⅔ cup butter, softened
1½ teaspoons rum
1½ teaspoons vanilla extract
6 cups confectioners' sugar
1 egg white, slightly beaten
3 to 6 tablespoons half-and-half

1. Cream butter, rum, and vanilla extract. Gradually add confectioners' sugar, creaming until fluffy after each addition.
2. Stir in egg white and blend in half-and-half, a tablespoon at a time, until frosting is desired consistency.

Enough to frost and decorate a Zuppa Inglese

Seven-Minute Frosting (*Ghiacciata Sette-Minuti*)

2 egg whites
1½ cups sugar
⅓ cup water
1 tablespoon light corn syrup
1 teaspoon vanilla extract
⅛ teaspoon salt

1. Combine all ingredients in the top of a double boiler; mix well.
2. Place over simmering water. Immediately and constantly beat with rotary beater 7 to 10 minutes, or until mixture holds stiff peaks. Remove from heat.

Enough to frost and decorate a Zuppa Inglese

Whipped Cream *(Panna Montata)*

2 cups chilled whipping cream
6 tablespoons confectioners' sugar
2 teaspoons vanilla extract

1. Beat whipping cream, 1 cup at a time, in a chilled 1-quart bowl using chilled beaters. Beat until cream stands in peaks.
2. Put whipped cream into a large chilled bowl. Fold or beat confectioners' sugar and vanilla extract into whipped cream until blended.

4 cups whipped cream

Stuffed Peaches *(Pesche Ripiene)*

½ cup blanched almonds, finely chopped
½ cup macaroon crumbs (see Note)
¼ cup sugar
1 tablespoon chopped candied orange peel
6 large firm peaches
⅓ cup sherry or Marsala

1. Combine almonds, macaroon crumbs, 2 tablespoons sugar, and orange peel; set aside.
2. Peel peaches, cut in half, and remove pits. Lightly fill peach halves with almond mixture. Put two halves together and secure with wooden picks. Place in a 10×6-inch baking dish, pour sherry over peaches, and sprinkle with remaining sugar.
3. Bake at 350°F 15 minutes. Serve either hot or cold.

6 servings

Note: To make macaroon crumbs, grind enough Macaroons (below) in electric blender to make ½ cup crumbs.

Queen's Biscuits *(Biscotti di Regina)*

4 cups sifted all-purpose flour
1 cup sugar
1 tablespoon baking powder
¼ teaspoon salt
1 cup shortening
2 eggs, slightly beaten
½ cup milk
⅔ to ¾ cup sesame seed

1. Combine flour, sugar, baking powder, and salt in a mixing bowl. Cut in shortening with a pastry blender or two knives until pieces are the size of small peas.
2. Stir in eggs and milk, one tablespoon at a time. Mix together thoroughly to make a soft dough.
3. Break off small pieces of dough, and roll between palms of hands to form rolls about 1½ inches long. Flatten slightly and roll in sesame seed. Place about ¾ inch apart on lightly greased cookie sheets.
4. Bake at 375°F 12 to 15 minutes, or until cookies are lightly browned.

About 6 dozen cookies

Macaroons *(Amaretti)*

¾ cup whole blanched almonds
2 egg whites
¼ teaspoon salt
1 cup sugar
½ teaspoon almond extract

1. Using an electric blender or nut grinder, finely grind almonds; set aside.
2. Beat egg whites with salt until frothy. Beat in sugar, 1 tablespoon at a time, beating thoroughly after each addition. Continue beating until stiff peaks are formed.
3. Fold in ground almonds with almond extract. Drop by teaspoonfuls about 1 inch apart on unglazed paper (baking parchment or brown) on a cookie sheet.
4. Bake at 350°F about 20 minutes, or until very lightly browned.

About 3 dozen macaroons

Apple Tart *(Torta di Mele)*

½ cup butter
1 teaspoon grated lemon peel
1 teaspoon lemon juice
½ cup sugar
4 egg yolks, well beaten
2 cups all-purpose flour
¼ teaspoon salt
⅛ teaspoon baking soda
4 egg whites
½ teaspoon vanilla extract
⅔ cup sugar
¾ cup walnuts, finely chopped
2 large apples, coarsely shredded

1. Cream butter with lemon peel and juice. Gradually add ½ cup sugar, creaming well. Add egg yolks in halves, beating well after each addition.
2. Blend flour, salt, and baking soda. Add in thirds to creamed mixture, beating until blended after each addition. Chill thoroughly.
3. Beat egg whites with vanilla extract until frothy. Gradually add the ⅔ cup sugar, beating well; continue beating until stiff peaks are formed. Fold in nuts and apples.
4. Roll out two thirds of the dough and line bottom of a 13×9-inch baking pan. Turn nut-apple mixture into pan and spread evenly into corners.
5. Roll pieces of remaining dough into pencil-thin strips and arrange lattice-fashion over top. Press strips slightly into filling.
6. Bake at 325°F 35 to 40 minutes, or until lightly browned. Set aside on rack to cool completely. Cut into squares and, if desired, serve topped with small scoops of vanilla ice cream.

One 13×9-inch tart

St. Joseph's Day Cream Puffs *(Zeppole di San Giuseppe)*

1 cup hot water
½ cup butter
1 tablespoon sugar
½ teaspoon salt
1 cup sifted all-purpose flour
4 eggs
1 teaspoon grated orange peel
1 teaspoon grated lemon peel
Ricotta filling (page 93; use one-half recipe)

1. Combine water, butter, sugar, and salt in a saucepan; bring to boiling. Add flour, all at once, and beat vigorously with a wooden spoon until mixture leaves the sides of pan and forms a smooth ball (about 3 minutes). Remove from heat.
2. Quickly beat in eggs one at a time, beating until smooth after each one is added. Continue beating until mixture is smooth and glossy. Add orange and lemon peel; mix thoroughly. Drop by tablespoonfuls 2 inches apart on a lightly greased baking sheet.
3. Bake at 450°F 15 minutes. Turn oven control to 350°F and bake 15 to 20 minutes, or until golden. Cool on wire racks.
4. To serve, cut a slit in side of each puff and fill with ricotta filling.

About 18 puffs

Note: If desired, puffs may be filled with Whipped Cream (page 89) or Pineapple Cream Filling (page 88).

Spumone

½ cup sugar
⅛ teaspoon salt
1 cup milk, scalded
3 egg yolks, beaten
1 cup whipping cream
½ ounce (½ square) unsweetened
    chocolate, melted
2 teaspoons rum extract
1 tablespoon sugar
⅛ teaspoon pistachio extract
2 drops green food coloring
½ cup whipping cream, whipped
1 maraschino cherry
1 tablespoon sugar
6 unblanched almonds, finely
    chopped
¼ teaspoon almond extract
½ cup whipping cream, whipped

1. Stir ½ cup sugar and salt into scalded milk in the top of a double boiler. Stir until sugar is dissolved.
2. Stir about 3 tablespoons of the hot milk into the egg yolks. Immediately return to double boiler top. Cook over boiling water, stirring constantly, about 5 minutes, or until mixture coats a spoon. Remove from heat and cool.
3. Stir in 1 cup whipping cream and divide mixture equally into two bowls.
4. Add melted chocolate to mixture in one bowl and mix thoroughly. Set in refrigerator.
5. Add rum extract to remaining mixture and pour into refrigerator tray. Freeze until mushy.
6. Turn into a chilled bowl and beat until mixture is smooth and creamy. Spoon into a chilled 1-quart mold and freeze until firm.
7. Fold 1 tablespoon sugar, pistachio extract, and food coloring into ½ cup whipping cream, whipped. Spoon over firm rum ice cream; freeze until firm.
8. When pistachio cream becomes firm, place the maraschino cherry in the center and return to freezer.
9. Fold 1 tablespoon sugar, chopped almonds, and almond extract into remaining ½ cup whipping cream, whipped. Spoon over firm pistachio cream. Freeze until firm.
10. When almond cream is firm, pour chocolate ice cream mixture into refrigerator tray and freeze until mushy.
11. Turn into a chilled bowl and beat until mixture is smooth and creamy. Spoon mixture over firm almond cream. Cover mold with aluminum foil or waxed paper. Return to freezer and freeze 6 to 8 hours, or until very firm.
12. To unmold, quickly dip mold into warm water and invert. Cut spumone into wedge-shaped pieces.

6 to 8 servings

Rum Cream (Mascarpone in Coppe)

2 packages (3 ounces each) cream
    cheese, softened
3 egg yolks
⅓ cup sugar
2 tablespoons rum
    Ladyfingers

1. Beat cream cheese until very light and fluffy; set aside.
2. Combine egg yolks and sugar, beating until very thick. Thoroughly blend in rum.
3. Pour egg-yolk mixture over cream cheese and fold in gently.
4. Fill 4 champagne or wine glasses to within ½ inch of rim. Chill 2 hours. Serve with ladyfingers.

4 servings

Marsala Custard *(Zabaglione)*

6 egg yolks
½ cup sugar
⅛ teaspoon salt
1 cup Marsala

1. In a bowl, beat egg yolks with sugar and salt until lemon colored. Stir in Marsala.
2. Cook in double boiler over simmering water. Beat constantly with rotary beater until mixture foams up and begins to thicken.
3. Turn into sherbet glasses and chill until serving time.

About 6 servings

Cheese and Fruit *(Formaggio e Frutta)*

Although used in many entrées, cheese is the most popular of Italian desserts whether served alone or accompanied by sweet, succulent fruits. An Italian family dinner usually is ended with fruit, cheese, and black coffee. Following are a few Italian dessert cheeses with a short description of each and the typical fruit they would usually accompany.

Bel Paese—a soft, mild cheese of the North and often served with ripe cherries or plums.

Gorgonzola—the most popular of the dessert cheeses, a creamy, tangy cheese veined with green mold; often served with sliced fresh pears, ripe Italian bananas, or quartered apples.

Stracchino—a tangy goat's milk cheese of Milan which may be accompanied by any number of fruits including peaches and grapes.

Provolone—whether the pear-shape Provolone, round Provolette, or sausage-shape Provolone salami, this is a favorite when accompanied by quartered apples and small slices of watermelon.

Caciocavallo—typifying a tapering beet root, this smoked cheese is delicious when served as a dessert with small crackers.

Ricotta—a soft, bland pot cheese often used in baking, this can be served as a dessert when accompanied by berries and figs.

Ricotta Pie (Torta di Ricotta)

Pastry:
- 2 cups all-purpose flour
- ½ teaspoon salt
- 1 cup shortening
- 2 egg yolks, slightly beaten
- 1 to 2 tablespoons cold water

Filling:
- 1½ pounds ricotta
- ¼ cup flour
- 2 tablespoons grated orange peel
- 2 tablespoons grated lemon peel
- 1 tablespoon vanilla extract
- ⅛ teaspoon salt
- 4 eggs
- 1 cup sugar
- 2 tablespoons confectioners' sugar

1. To make pastry, combine flour with salt. Cut in shortening with a pastry blender until it is the size of small peas. Gradually sprinkle egg yolks over mixture; mix until thoroughly combined. Stir in just enough water to hold dough together.

2. Shape pastry into a ball and flatten on a lightly floured surface. Roll out to form a circle about 11 inches in diameter and ⅛ inch thick. Fit dough into a 9-inch round layer cake pan. (Handle dough carefully as it breaks easily.) Trim dough, leaving a ½-inch border around top of pan. Pinch dough between index finger and thumb to make it stand about ¼ inch high around edge; set aside.

3. For filling, combine cheese, flour, orange peel, lemon peel, vanilla extract, and salt; set aside. Beat eggs until foamy. Gradually add sugar, and continue beating until eggs are thick and pile softly. Stir eggs into ricotta mixture until well blended and smooth. Pour filling into pastry.

4. Bake at 350°F about 50 to 60 minutes, or until filling is firm and pastry is golden brown. Cool on wire rack. Sift confectioners' sugar over top before serving.

8 to 10 servings

Neapolitan Fondant Roll (Fondante Napoletana)

- 1 egg white
- 3 cups confectioners' sugar
- 1 teaspoon vanilla extract
- 4 tablespoons unsalted butter, softened
- 3 drops red food coloring
- 3 drops green food coloring
- ½ cup finely chopped toasted almonds

1. Beat egg white until it forms soft peaks. Sift confectioners' sugar into egg white and combine thoroughly. Add vanilla extract; mix well. Cream butter until it is fluffy, add to the sugar mixture, and beat mixture until it is as fluffy as possible.

2. Divide creamed mixture into 3 equal parts. Blend red food coloring into one part, green into another, and leave remaining part white. Chill in refrigerator until firm enough to handle (about 1 hour).

3. With a spatula that has been dipped in cold water, shape the green part into a 7×3-inch rectangle on a piece of waxed paper. Spread the white part on the green, and the red on the white, forming a rectangle about ½ inch thick.

4. Using waxed paper, roll up rectangle from wide edge into a roll with the green on the outside. Chill 30 minutes, unwrap, and coat well with nuts. Rewrap in waxed paper, and chill in refrigerator 12 hours.

5. To serve, remove paper and cut in ¼-inch slices.

About 40 slices

Index